Theos Friends' Prog

Theos is a public theology think tank which seeks
about the role of faith and belief in society.

We were launched in November 2006 with the sup...........Archbishop of
Canterbury, Dr Rowan Williams, and the Cardinal Archbishop of Westminster,
Cardinal Cormac Murphy-O'Connor.

We provide

- high-quality research, reports and publications;
- an events programme;
- news, information and analysis to media companies
  and other opinion formers.

We can only do this with your help!

Theos Friends receive complimentary copies of all Theos publications,
invitations to selected events and monthly email bulletins.

If you would like to become a Friend, please detach or photocopy the form
below, and send it with a cheque to Theos for £60.

Thank you.

Yes, I would like to help change public opinion!
I enclose a cheque for **£60** made payable to Theos.

Name

Address

Postcode

Email

Tel

Data Protection Theos will use your personal data to inform you of its activities.
If you prefer not to receive this information please tick here ☐

By completing you are consenting to receiving communications by telephone and email.
Theos will not pass on your details to any third party.

Please return this form to:
Theos | 77 Great Peter Street | London | SW1P 2EZ
S: 97711:   D: 36701:

The public theology think tank

Theos

The public theology think tank

what Theos is

Theos is a public theology think tank which exists to undertake research and provide commentary on social and political arrangements. We aim to impact opinion around issues of faith and belief in society. We were launched in November 2006 with the support of the Archbishop of Canterbury, Dr Rowan Williams, and the Cardinal Archbishop of Westminster, Cardinal Cormac Murphy-O'Connor. Our first report *"Doing God": A Future for Faith in the Public Square* examined the reasons why faith will play an increasingly significant role in public life.

what Theos stands for

Society is embarking on a process of de-secularisation. Interest in spirituality is increasing across Western culture. Faith is on the agenda of both government and the media. In the arts, humanities and social sciences there are important intellectual developments currently taking place around questions of values and identity. Theos speaks into this new context. Our perspective is that faith is not just important for human flourishing and the renewal of society, but that society can only truly flourish if faith is given the space to do so. We reject notions of a sacred-secular divide.

what Theos works on

Theos undertakes research across a wide range of subject areas. We analyse social and political change and offer interesting new angles and alternative perspectives on the issues that matter.

what Theos provides

Theos provides:

- a research and publishing programme,
- conferences, seminars and lectures,
- outreach to university, college and school students,
- news, information and analysis to media companies and other opinion formers, with a one-stop information line available to journalists,
- regular email bulletins,
- other related activities.

In addition to our independently driven work, Theos provides research, analysis and advice to individuals and organisations across the private, public and not-for-profit sectors. Our unique position within the think tank sector means that we have the capacity to develop proposals that carry values - with an eye to demonstrating what really works. Our staff and consultants have strong public affairs experience, an excellent research track record and a high level of theological literacy. We are practised in campaigning, media relations, detailed policy development and effecting policy change.

www.theosthinktank.co.uk

Turbulent Priests?

The Archbishop of Canterbury in contemporary English politics

Daniel Gover

Published by Theos in 2011

© Theos

For further information and subscription details please contact:

Theos
Licence Department
77 Great Peter Street
London
SW1P 2EZ

T 020 7828 7777
E hello@theosthinktank.co.uk
www.theosthinktank.co.uk

contents

acknowledgements

This report is based on the research I carried out for my MPhil dissertation, and over the course of the two projects I have been in contact with a number of people who have greatly assisted me in my work. In particular, I would like to thank George Carey (Archbishop of Canterbury, 1991-2002) and Rowan Williams (Archbishop of Canterbury, 2002-present), both of whom were extraordinarily generous in agreeing to make time in their busy schedules to meet with me during my original project. Whilst converting it into this report, Nick Spencer has been an invaluable source of advice and encouragement and his comments on successive drafts have markedly improved the final text. I would also like to acknowledge with thanks the assistance of: Jonathan Chaplin, Helen Dawes, Pieter van Houten, Graham Howes, Kenneth Medhurst, Andrew Partington and Stephen Timms, as well as Lambeth Palace library and the Parliamentary Archives.

Finally, I would like to take this opportunity to record my gratitude to Dr Emile Perreau-Saussine, who was originally my dissertation supervisor at The University of Cambridge. Emile suggested the topic of my research and was hugely encouraging as I began working on it. His unexpected death in February 2010, aged 37, was a great loss to all who knew him. It is to his memory that I dedicate this report.

foreword

Archbishop of Canterbury makes a valuable contribution to the nation's political life" is not a claim calculated to grab headlines, particularly when made by a think tank originally set up with the encouragement of the Archbishop of Canterbury. You would not need to be a member of the National Secular Society to respond, "Well, they would say that, wouldn't they?"

Theos (whose inaugural report did indeed bear a foreword jointly written by the Archbishops of Canterbury and Westminster) has a particular interest in the interface of politics and the Christian faith. It keenly advocates an active and open Christian presence in British public life (provided it is also suitably thoughtful and reasonable). And it has often drawn on Anglican (as well as Catholic and evangelical) social teaching to inform its publications. Hence it is not ideally placed to conduct a wholly disinterested empirical study of the nature and success (or otherwise) of that Christian presence.

It is for that reason that whenever Theos does engage in such empirical studies, we do so through the work and in the company of independent academics. *Coming off the Bench,* a study of Episcopal parliamentary activity during the Thatcher and Blair years was based on the doctoral research of Andrew Partington. *Mapping the Field,* a review of current research evidence on the impact of schools with a Christian ethos, was conducted by the academic Elizabeth Green. So it is with *Turbulent Priests?* This report began life as an MPhil dissertation, submitted to the Department of Politics and International Studies at The University of Cambridge, exploring the political behaviour of the Archbishop of Canterbury in England between 1979 and 2010, and it retains several marks of this early life.

It is, for example, meticulously detailed. As he explains in his introduction, Daniel Gover has been through a huge number and range of archiepiscopal political interventions, whether in speeches, articles, media appearances, or parliamentary debates. He has examined a great deal of press coverage of these interventions, from supportive *Guardian* editorials to antagonistic *Daily Mail* columns (and vice versa). And he has been careful to locate all these debates within the public opinion of the time, using British Social Attitudes, the European Values Study and Ipsos MORI as his guide. The length of chapter three and the sheer number of footnotes is testimony to the determination to establish precisely what the archbishop said, on what subject, in what context and with what response. If we are to assess the value of archiepiscopal politics, it is vital to do this empirical spadework and to do it well.

Turbulent Priests? is not simply an exercise in reportage, however. The main purpose of the report is to assess the value of archiepiscopal politics or, more precisely, to assess which of the various verdicts on archiepiscopal politics is most accurate. Gover has taken care to convey clearly and fairly what the objections to archiepiscopal political activity have been over the last thirty years, no matter how hostile. These have frequently been voiced by the same newspapers that reported on that activity but have also been comprehensively and forcefully articulated most often by the National Secular Society (NSS). While it may seem odd for a Christian think tank to praise the NSS, in this instance it needs to be recognised that the range and vigour of its statements on Christian political activity crystallise the general objections to that activity both clearly and helpfully.

These objections are that that the Archbishop's promotion of the common good is compromised by his pursuit of the Church's institutional interests, or that his moral perspectives are outdated and unrepresentative of contemporary public opinion, or that his input is irrelevant and adds little to mainstream political debate. Such criticisms have been applied frequently to archiepiscopal interventions, sometimes in a rather frenzied and haphazard manner, but also often in precise and targeted ways. Thus, his statements on asylum have been out-of-step with the public (as the public opinion data broadly confirm); his statements on climate change have added little to similar but more expert opinions on the topic; and his statements on religious legislation have been self-serving, etc. However one may instinctively view these subjects or the Archbishop's intervention in them, there is a charge sheet to answer.

Against such objections stands the opposing view, one that has apparently been held by Robert Runcie, George Carey and Rowan Williams themselves, that the Archbishop's contribution to British political life has been to promote the common good by articulating moral concerns in an authentic (and sometimes also distinctive) Christian voice. Archiepiscopal participation in political debate helps lift that debate, however briefly, above the short-term and partisan, and (changing metaphors) ground it in more substantial (and often more accessible) ethical considerations. Without wishing to spoil the plot, Gover concludes that while some of the accusations stick in some particular policy areas, the Archbishop's assessment of his own contribution is largely correct. His presence in British political life over the last thirty years has been to open up debate to questions of what it means to be human.

The reader will, of course, be the judge of how defensible is that conclusion but it is worth reflecting, as Gover does briefly in his final chapter, on what are the consequences if it is justifiable. Writing of Winston Churchill's religion, the historian Paul Addison one remarked that the great man "belonged to an era of secularised religion in which the doctrines of liberalism, socialism and imperialism were all bathed in the afterglow of a Christian sunset. Now the afterglow has gone: and political discourse has shrunk into a narrow, stultifying recital of economic indicators, enlivened by occasional outbreaks of xenophobia."[1]

Allowing for the hyperbole, this is not an unreasonable assessment of much political debate today. A sense of frustration and disenchantment hovers around contemporary British politics – both among politicians and voters. Most recognise that a healthy national political life demands more than the reporting of quarterly growth figures and the wrangling of realpolitik. Even if opening up political debates to the wider questions of human purpose, identity and dignity will rarely decide them, it will nevertheless serve to ground and deepen them. If this report's analysis of archiepiscopal political activity is right, the Archbishop's presence in public life over recent decades has done just that. That does not, of course, constitute a knock-down argument for establishment or indeed for any particular ecclesiastical participation in politics. But it does suggest that there is a genuine and profound value to this curious theo-political figure that we would do well to recognise. Perhaps the message of this report is that we need to appreciate what we have got. But then, Theos would say that.

Nick Spencer
Research Director, Theos

foreword reference

1. Paul Addison, 'The religion of Winston Churchill', in *Public and Private Doctrine: Essays in British History Presented to Maurice Cowling*, Michael Bentley (ed.) (Cambridge, 1993) p. 250.

introduction

"The Archbishop's speech is, at base, self-serving and dangerously illiberal."[1] "[T]he Church of England can look back with real gratitude to the national pronouncements of Robert Runcie."[2] "The Archbishop of Canterbury spoke of our duty to the environment – no surprise there from a self-confessed 'bearded lefty.'"[3] "Dr Carey was here speaking with uncharacteristic firmness and subtlety to zealots in both parties."[4] "[T]hat pathetic weather-vane windbag, the Archbishop of Canterbury, has now dithered his way into the debate."[5] "[T]he Archbishop of Canterbury [...has] sat on the fence so long that rust is beginning to set in."[6] "The Archbishop of Canterbury is to be congratulated for firmly condemning adultery."[7] "The whole nation is appalled, outraged and incredulous that Rowan Williams should come out with such dangerous claptrap."[8] "[I]f the Archbishop – and sadly other church leaders – are so clearly out of tune with the vast majority of their fellow countrymen, is it any wonder that so few go to church nowadays?"[9] "[This was] a magnificently clear and assured debut on the national stage from a man who is already playing a compelling role in national debate."[10] "Do we have to wait until the hate-filled mobs storm into Canterbury Cathedral and drag him from the pulpit before the Archbishop of Canterbury grasps that Christianity is in danger in this country?"[11]

The Archbishop of Canterbury is a political figure to be reckoned with. He speaks out frequently and on a wide range of issues. And if this selection of reactions to his various political interventions over the last thirty years is to be believed, he excites a very wide range of reactions.

Every Archbishop of Canterbury in history has worked closely with the powers that be, and many have antagonised them. Although few have suffered the fate of Thomas Becket (murdered in his cathedral in 1170) or Thomas Cranmer (executed in Oxford in 1556), the nature and value of the Archbishop's political role continues to be disputed.

The Archbishop's political functions are rooted in the Church's centuries-old status as the official (or established) religion of England. England's head of state continues to be the Supreme Governor of the Church of England, whom the Archbishop crowns during a coronation service saturated in Christian language and imagery. The canon law of the Church remains an official component of English law and must be rubber-stamped by Parliament. The monarch, acting on the advice of the Prime Minister, retains the right to appoint to key positions in the Church, including the Archbishop of Canterbury, although in recent decades the Sovereign's choice has become progressively restricted. The Church's most substantive privilege is the right for 26 of its most senior bishops to speak and to vote in the House of Lords.

The Archbishop of Canterbury is not, of course, primarily a political figure. A recent review of the office, published in 2001 and led by the former Home Secretary, Douglas Hurd, identified six distinct roles: Diocesan Bishop of Canterbury; Metropolitan for the Southern Province of the Church of England (giving him authority over 30 dioceses mostly in the south of England); Primate of All England (making him the most senior bishop in the Church of England); leader of the Anglican Communion (a loose affiliation of Anglican churches worldwide with approximately 77 million adherents); an ecumenical figure in relation to other Christian churches; and a Christian leader with interfaith responsibilities. It is as Primate of All England that most of the Archbishop's political interventions are made.[12]

> *The fact of the Archbishop's political intervention is not under debate. What is disputed is whether his input into political debate is of any value in a 21st century and increasingly plural England.*

Despite this rather crowded job description, the Archbishop's political engagement is a central component of his work and is today exercised primarily through participation in political debate. This can take a number of forms, from speeches (including in the House of Lords and in the Church's legislature, the General Synod), to media interviews, press statements, and even direct lobbying. Whatever else one may say of them, the Archbishop's political comments are not usually considered irrelevant. Analysis of the pages of *The Guardian* – hardly a stronghold of religious traditionalism – over the past three decades reveals that the Archbishop's comments have been reported on a bewilderingly wide range of topics, including nuclear disarmament, the Iraq war, the funding of the BBC, capital punishment, the National Health Service, the miners' strike, trade unionism, international development, and the age of consent for gay men. The Archbishop also retains sufficient access to raise matters with the government away from the glare of the media spotlight. When early in his tenure George Carey requested a meeting with a Cabinet minister about the government's immigration policy, he was surprised to discover that it was the minister who travelled to meet him.[13]

As such, the fact of the Archbishop's political intervention is not under debate. What is disputed is whether his input into political debate is of any value in a 21st Century and increasingly plural England. It is this question that forms the focus of this report.

turbulent priests?

This study is an empirical evaluation of the contribution that the Archbishop of Canterbury made to politics in England between 1980 and 2010. Although much of the data are also relevant to the other countries of the United Kingdom, the focus is on England because the Church of England is the established church only in that country.[14]

The time period of the study begins on 25 February 1980, when Robert Runcie formally became the 102nd Archbishop of Canterbury. The closing date is taken as 11 May 2010, when Gordon Brown resigned as the British Prime Minister. During this period, three individuals held the office of Archbishop of Canterbury: Robert Runcie (1980-1991), George Carey (1991-2002) and Rowan Williams (from 2002). Over the same period, the political landscape shifted significantly and can be divided into two distinct periods: the Conservative years, under Margaret Thatcher (1979-1990) and John Major (1990-1997); and the Labour years, under Tony Blair (1997-2007) and Gordon Brown (2007-2010).

The study is based on extensive research from a wide range of sources. A large number of transcripts of speeches by the three officeholders have been analysed, along with biographies and autobiographies about them and other political figures. Interviews have been conducted with the only two living individuals to have held the post of Archbishop – George Carey and Rowan Williams – although only content from the former is explicitly referred to in the body of the report. Newspaper articles and other media content have been consulted, both to provide a record of the Archbishop's activity over the period and to assess how it was perceived and reported. This evidence is supplemented with public opinion data from the British Social Attitudes survey and from the European Values Study.[15]

Although much of the available opinion data relate to Britain as a whole, it is assumed that in most cases it is also representative of England. The extent to which we can believe such opinion polls is, of course, a matter for debate. Secondary sources, including academic studies, have also been used.

Some key terms in the report are used with specific meanings. Politics is loosely defined to refer to anything that is connected to the operation of the English state, although the focus is on public policy. The primary subject of the study is the office of the Archbishop of Canterbury, but it is often also necessary to refer to the individual officeholders. In order to distinguish clearly between the two, Archbishop (along with the generic he) is used to refer to the office of the Archbishop of Canterbury,[16] whereas officeholder is used whenever the focus is on a particular individual who has held the post. When capitalised, Church refers to the Church of England, whereas the lowercase church is used for all other Christian churches and for individual congregations.

In chapter one, the Archbishop's engagement in politics is considered from a theoretical perspective. The chapter begins by locating the topic in its historical context and introducing the three officeholders. It then sets out four theoretical understandings of the Archbishop's political engagement. The first is a positive assessment based on the officeholders' own statements about their role: that the Archbishop seeks to promote the common good by voicing Christian moral concerns. Against this view, three counter-claims are identified: that the Archbishop's promotion of the common good is compromised by his pursuit of the Church's institutional interests; that the Archbishop's moral perspectives are outdated and unrepresentative; and that his input is irrelevant and adds little to mainstream political debate.

Against these four perspectives, chapter two assesses evidence of how the Archbishop has actually engaged in politics over this period. Eight policy areas are considered in turn. The first section considers the Archbishop's approach to urban poverty and, in particular, focuses on a series of reports on the topic beginning with *Faith in the City* in 1985. This is followed by a section on his engagement with asylum and immigration legislation, including the British Nationality Bill in 1981 and the Asylum and Immigration Bill in 1996, and then a section about his support for the reform of the criminal justice system. The fourth section considers the Archbishop's stance towards British involvement in military conflict around the world, and focuses on four major conflicts during this period: the Falklands war of 1982, the Gulf war of 1991, the Afghanistan invasion of 2001, and the Iraq war beginning in 2003. Attention then turns to a second international issue, that of the environment and climate change, which has seen increased levels of archiepiscopal activism over the course of this period.

The final three sections consider policy areas in which the three objections are expected to be particularly applicable. The Archbishop is expected to be especially out of line with popular opinion over traditional moral issues (section six), which comprise issues relating to sexual relationships and the sanctity of life. This is followed by a section on children and education policy, with the main focus on areas in which the Church has clear institutional interests: its extensive network of publicly-funded schools, and the teaching and observance of religion in England's schools. The final section considers a cluster of public policy issues that relate to religion, including blasphemy legislation, religious exemptions from the law, and the public financing of religious groups. Although it is not possible in a report of this length to provide a comprehensive account of the Archbishop's political activity, this selection of issues is sufficiently representative to allow an accurate evaluation of his contribution to political debate.

On the basis of this detailed analysis, chapter three draws conclusions about the Archbishop's contribution to politics over this period. The chapter begins by considering each of the three objections in turn and assessing the extent to which they are plausible in the light of the evidence. In the light of this analysis, it then returns to the Archbishop's own, positive, assessment of his political role, and draws some conclusions about the extent to which he did indeed succeed in articulating a valuable moral voice in support of the common good. Based on these assessments of the Archbishop's activity, the report concludes by considering the implications of its findings for the future of archiepiscopal political activity, not least for the continued establishment of the Church of England.

introduction references

1. Terry Sanderson, cit. in "Archbishop's Call For More Law to Protect Religion is 'Self-Serving and Dangerous'," National Secular Society, 30 January 2008,
http://www.secularism.org.uk/archbishopscallformorelawtoprote.html.

2. Hugh Montefiore, "In Mrs Thatcher's Britain," *in Robert Runcie: A Portrait by His Friends,* ed. David L Edwards (London: HarperCollins, 1990), p. 84.

3. Giles Fraser, "A Very Lefty Festival," 27 December 2007, *The Guardian,*
http://www.guardian.co.uk/commentisfree/2007/dec/27/religion.world.

4. "Dr Carey's Faith in Society," 6 October 1992, *The Independent.*

5. Polly Toynbee, "A Woman's Supreme Right Over Her Own Body is In Jeopardy," 26 October 2007, *The Guardian,*
http://www.guardian.co.uk/commentisfree/2007/oct/26/comment.politics.

6. Bruce Kent cit. in John McGhie, "Anti-War Coalitions Forged in Wave of Rallies," 27 January 1991, *The Observer.*

7. "Home Truths About Sex," 18 January 1994, *The Daily Mail.*

8. "Rowan Going," 9 February 2008, *The Sun.*

9. "Out of Tune With the People," 28 July 1982, *The Sun.*

10. "Premier and Prelate: Blair and Williams Test the Limits," 20 December 2002, *The Guardian,*
http://www.guardian.co.uk/politics/2002/dec/20/publicservices.labour.

11. Peter Hitchens, "Our Nice, Furry Archbishop... Lost in a Barbarous World," 4 April 2010, *The Mail on Sunday,*
http://hitchensblog.mailonsunday.co.uk/2010/04/our-nice-furry-archbishop-lost-in-a-barbarous-world-.html.

12. *To Lead and to Serve: The Report of the Review of the See of Canterbury:* A Report to the Most Revd and Rt Hon Dr George Carey by the Review Team Chaired by the Rt Hon the Lord Hurd of Westwell CH CBE (London: Church House, 2001).

13. George Carey to author, House of Lords, 3 May 2010.

14. The Anglican churches in Wales and Ireland – the Church of Wales and the Church of Ireland – are both disestablished. The Church of Scotland is Presbyterian.

15. British Social Attitudes data accessed at www.britsocat.com, and European Values Study data accessed at www.jdsurvey.net/evs. In both cases, respondents who gave no response are included in the proportions cited. For all other poll data, headline figures are used.

16. Except where another archdiocese is specified, such as for the Archbishop of York (the second most senior bishop in the Church of England) or the Archbishop of Westminster (the leader of the Roman Catholic Church in England and Wales).

claiming the moral high ground: archiepiscopal politics in theory

In order to appreciate the Archbishop's understanding of his political role, it is important first to grasp the historic connections between Church and state in England. As was noted in the introduction, these interactions date back hundreds of years. The most significant turning point was the Reformation, when the Church broke away from Rome and the English monarch became its Supreme Governor. As a result of this, the Church became closely associated with "understandings of the British national identity [...] that stress English society's organic unity".[1] The establishment of the Church continues to give its leaders a sense of pastoral responsibility for the wellbeing of the nation. It also seems likely that the Church's parish structure, which covers the entire country, enhances this sense of responsibility as well as giving it first-hand understanding of living conditions in every part of the nation.

The Church's established status leads it to perform a range of functions that could be described as political. One of these – although not a focus of this report – is the Church's capacity to respond, on behalf of the state, to the more "sacred" moments in national life, most notably death.[2] Out of 54 House of Lords debates in which the Archbishop participated during this period, around 15 percent were expressive of national or international mourning, and almost a tenth were on topics of national celebration.[3] The same characteristics have been picked up in studies of churches elsewhere. For example, a study of the Catholic churches in Latin Europe suggests that, both by articulating these moments of national mourning and by participating in political policy debate (such as through lobbying), the churches "see[k] to change the terms of the political debate by opening it up to the larger question of being".[4] The Archbishop of Canterbury's political motivations may be understood in a very similar way: both in detailed policy debate and at times of national mourning or celebration, he aims to open up politics to larger "ontological" questions of what it means to be human.

In recent times, the Church has not participated in politics in an overtly partisan fashion. During the period studied in this report, the Archbishop worked with and criticised politicians from across the political spectrum. In a joint letter issued prior to the 2001 general election, the Archbishops of Canterbury and York were careful to emphasise their nonpartisan motivations: "Categorically, we make no covert appeal to you to vote for one party or another."[5] Runcie caused a minor controversy when he voted in the 1983 general election – most members of the House of Lords are not entitled to vote – particularly when rumours surfaced that he had cast his vote for the Social Democrats.[6]

To analyse the Archbishop's activity, it is necessary to have some understanding of the three personalities that occupied Augustine's chair during the period. The first was Robert Runcie (February 1980 – January 1991), theologically a liberal Anglo-Catholic and politically centrist.[7] His approach to the role was particularly influenced by his close relationships with the political establishment: as a younger man he had crossed paths with several people who went on to hold senior political positions during his archiepiscopate. Runcie was succeeded by George Carey (March 1991 – October 2002), an evangelical with working class roots, though again politically centrist and nonpartisan.[8] As the Archbishop during a period of huge growth in mass communication, Carey's roots and common touch made his political comment perhaps the most easily accessible of the three. The final office holder during the period was Rowan Williams (December 2002 – present), a Welsh Anglo-Catholic and a former member of the Labour Party.[9] One of his distinctive qualities has been a particularly intellectual and philosophical approach, which reflects his background as a distinguished Oxbridge theologian.

All three men strongly advocated the Church's political engagement on the basis of the holistic nature of the Christian faith. Runcie claimed that the Christian message has a "social facet" that makes political engagement a legitimate function of the Church.[10] Carey likewise argued that the Church's political responsibility arises directly from the Christian faith: "a Christianity which is not concerned about the whole of life is not a Christianity I want or the modern world deserves."[11] In Williams' estimation, "there is no way in which a Church can be indifferent to politics if politics is understood as that science of understanding and managing with justice the way human beings live together."[12]

Although all three took seriously the office's political responsibilities, it is possible to discern some differences in the priority they gave to them, or at least in their approach. Appendix 1 sets out the intervention of the Archbishop in House of Lords debates during this period. The table identifies debates that were about the internal operation of the Church (usually legislation passed by the Church's General Synod) and tributes of mourning or celebration. Once these are excluded, 36 debates remain. Of these, Runcie was responsible for 15 (roughly one per 266 days of his tenure), Carey for 10 (one per 424 days), and Williams for 11 (one per 247 days). However, whereas 15 Lords votes cast by Runcie have been identified (one per 266 days), Carey appears to have cast seven including one on an internal Church matter (one per 605 days), and Williams just three (one per 906 days). It should be emphasised that these data provide only a rough indication of the Archbishop's political activity, as they give no account to the length or quality of the speeches, nor to tactical decisions such as the relative proportion of political activity conducted inside and outside the Lords. These caveats aside, the evidence suggests that the Archbishop may have been especially politically active during Runcie's tenure.

The Archbishop is arguably England's leading moral and religious leader. It is therefore remarkable how few studies are devoted to his involvement in politics,[13] although a small body of research exists about the contemporary political engagement of the Church as a whole.[14] One of the contributions of this report is to document the extent of the Archbishop's political intervention during this period. Yet the primary purpose of the report is to go beyond merely reporting his contribution to evaluating it. To this end, the remainder of this chapter sets out four theoretical assessments of the Archbishop's engagement in politics, the first section offering a positive hypothesis of the Archbishop's political engagement, and the second then identifying three critical perspectives.

a moral voice for the common good: a positive assessment

The first perspective on the Archbishop's involvement in English politics builds upon the Church's own understanding of its mission. Put simply, it is that the Archbishop seeks to make a valuable Christian moral input into public policy debate in support of the common good. When asked in interview to describe the political role of the Archbishop, Carey gave the following response:

> It's anchored into the wellbeing of a country, the nation, and no one who takes this job on is going to think of it simply as 'my major concern is the Church' or 'my major concern is my denomination'. It's far more complex than that and I think it's linked up with one's philosophy of the human being and the role of the Church in society.[15]

Without being prompted, Carey thus described the role in a way that emphasised the promotion of society's common good. Elsewhere, he indicated that this is connected to the Church's established status, which he claimed "underwrite[s] the commitment of a national church to serve the entire community".[16] In a speech delivered early in his archiepiscopate, Carey suggested that the role

The Archbishop seeks to make a valuable Christian moral input into public policy debate in support of the common good.

of the churches in politics "is to point to the eternal values and hopes which give humankind its distinctive focus".[17] He also proposed five guiding principles for Christian political action: a commitment to "eternal values, absolute standards of what is good"; offering a "long-term perspective" to balance the short-term electoral cycle; a commitment to freedom and justice for every individual; humility and tolerance of others; and participation in groups that occupy the space between the individual and the government, such as churches.[18] His emphasis on "absolute standards" reflects a particular concern he had about the privatisation of morality.

Both Runcie and Williams approached political activism from a similar perspective. When speaking about the Church's attitude to political power, Runcie often used the phrase "critical solidarity", by which he meant that the Church must support the principle of government whilst always holding it to a higher moral standard of right and wrong.[19] Elsewhere, he commented that the Church's established status places it "at the service of the whole nation".[20] Runcie outlined four principles that he claimed guided his own approach to political debate: "to unpack the moral principles involved in any issue"; to "speak up for the poor and the powerless"; to pay attention to the international dimensions of any issue; and "to strive for loyalty to truth, for sober, measured speech" rather than populist rhetoric.[21]

Although Williams has downplayed the role of providing "moral leadership", he nevertheless agreed that one of the Archbishop's roles is to articulate "some sort of moral vision that's communicable to the nation at large."[22] Unlike his two predecessors, he does not appear to have clearly set out the principles that guided his political activity. However, his letter to party leaders in advance of the 2005 general election reveals some of his priorities. In it, he outlined the moral dimensions of four mainstream issues – climate change, global economics, criminal justice, and children and young people – and argued that all were motivated by the Christian conviction "that the world is to be cherished, the innocent protected and human dignity preserved."[23] The positive assessment of the Archbishop's political role is therefore that he makes a valuable contribution to political debate by highlighting moral concerns in order to promote the common good.

morally compromised: three objections

Against this positive estimation of the Archbishop's role, a number of counter-claims can be made. It is not uncommon to hear it said, from both religious and secular perspectives, that religious leaders should refrain from politics. This somewhat vague assertion usually rests on a number of more reasoned concerns, three of which are particularly relevant. Although they do not necessarily provide an exhaustive critique of the Archbishop's involvement in politics over this period, they do represent the most significant objections.

The first objection is that the Archbishop's political engagement is *self-serving*, and that his claim to be a credible moral spokesman is undermined by his position at the head of a Church that has vested institutional interests. A number of academic studies by political scientists contend that the political behaviour of religious actors can often be explained by reference to their institutional interests, such as their membership levels, material resources, and social authority. Although their analysis is often highly nuanced, the central claim of these texts is that the political engagement of religious actors can often be understood as a way of furthering these interests, such as by lobbying for resources, attracting new adherents, or by competing against rival religions.[24] A less nuanced version of this analysis is often heard at a popular level by pressure groups that are sceptical about the merits of religious political activism. The National Secular Society (NSS) has, for instance, described the Archbishop's support for Church schools as "self-serving"[25] and "a cynical exercise in self-perpetuation".[26] When the House of Lords debated the Academies Bill in 2010, which included provisions relating to faith schools, the NSS commented that the Church's bishops "had little need to table their usual self-interested amendments".[27] In a submission about the reform of the House of Lords, the NSS argued that the Church's bishops in the Lords have used "their entrenched position of power and privilege to behave in self-serving ways".[28] Likewise, the British Humanist Association (BHA) suggested that the bishops "are likely to vote collectively in the interests of an external organisation – the Church of England – with its own agenda."[29] Although it is unlikely that these groups would dismiss *all* of the Archbishop's political involvement in this way, this objection is clearly central to their interpretation of the Archbishop's political participation.

This objection, in common with the Archbishop's own positive assessment of his political engagement, is concerned with questions of motivation: while the officeholders claim to be motivated by the common good, critics respond that they are in fact motivated by vested interests. In practice, it is exceptionally difficult to accurately determine an actor's motivations. Any political stance that is both popular and newsworthy could be regarded as self-interested, perhaps an attempt to attract new members to the Church, or to preserve and enhance its social authority. Given that there is evidence that religions that demand adherence to strict behavioural requirements tend to grow most rapidly,[30] even unpopular political stances could theoretically be accounted for in this way. Moreover, given that the Church is part of England's establishment, it is arguable that activity intended to further the common good is, by definition, self-interested. In other words, explanations based on self-interest can easily become tautological. Rather than become entangled in these complexities, this report is primarily concerned with direct and clear attempts to further the institutional interests of the Church itself. Based on empirical evidence of how the Archbishop has actually behaved, it assesses the extent to which institutional self-interest offers a more plausible explanation than moral altruism in each policy area.

The second objection is that the Archbishop's moral views are *outdated* or *unrepresentative*. It is often noted by opponents of religious politics that the level of religious participation and commitment has fallen over recent decades. According to data from the English Church Census, total Sunday attendance has fallen from almost five and a half million in 1979 to just over three million in 2005. Attendance at Church of England services reflects this downward trend, falling to less than one million in the 2005 English Church Census.[31] Noting this decline, the NSS commented, "[i]t is not tenable to suggest the Church speaks for the nation."[32] Perhaps because of this, *British Social Attitudes* data record that public opinion is largely unsupportive of religious leaders attempting to influence government decisions (although, as this report argues, popular sentiment is almost certainly more complex and discerning than this measure suggests).

This objection may be particularly relevant to those issues that are often referred to as "traditional moral issues," such as sexual relationships, abortion and euthanasia. In a column for the NSS, Terry Sanderson wrote that "the vast majority of the public oppose [Archbishop Rowan Williams'] views on topics such as faith schools and voluntary euthanasia."[33] The BHA took a similar line when it commented that "the Church's stance on issues such as gay equality, women's equality and reforming the law on assisted dying is not representative of even its own flock, let alone the rest of society."[34] In each of the policy areas considered in this report, the Archbishop's stance is therefore assessed against public opinion. A particularly common expression of this objection is the claim that religious spokesmen tend to be preoccupied with this narrow range of traditional moral issues at the expense of more mainstream concerns. In a 2007 column for *The Guardian*, Polly Toynbee observed that, far from "us[ing] their greatest firepower [...] to challenge gross inequality", religious groups are preoccupied with "other people's sexuality".[35] Writing in *The Independent*, Johann Hari claimed that the Church's bishops in the Lords "use their power to relentlessly fight against equality for women and gay people, and to deny you the right to choose a peaceful and dignified death when the time comes".[36] This report therefore assesses the extent to which these issues have preoccupied the Archbishop's political activism.

> Is the role played by the Archbishop of Canterbury best understood as a valuable moral voice that has contributed to the national (and even global) common good, or as a series of self-serving, outdated, unrepresentative, unnecessary, or irrelevant contributions?

The third objection is that the Archbishop's contribution is *unnecessary* or *irrelevant*, as other actors are amply capable of contributing moral perspectives to political debate. In a submission concerning the presence of the Church's bishops in a reformed House of Lords, the NSS wrote, "[w]e reject the implication that the Bishops somehow provide special moral insights denied to other members of the House."[37] In many cases, the argument is that religious leaders lack sufficiently distinctive moral insight to justify them being guaranteed seats in the Lords by virtue of their positions. This is not quite the same as claiming that the Archbishop's comments are never distinctive enough to justify attention. Yet the implication is surely that the added value brought by religious leaders to political debate is generally quite low. At times, political comments made outside the Lords by the Archbishop have attracted criticism on the same grounds. This appears to have been the contention of Terry Sanderson of the NSS, who remarked on a media interview given by Williams, "[y]ou could read any or all of these opinions just about any day of the week in the columns of newspapers [...] and none of them are particularly 'religious'. There wasn't a truly original insight anywhere in the whole interview."[38] (It is worth noting that this criticism is at least partially incompatible with the second objection, which is that the Archbishop's comments are out of step with society precisely *because* they are distinctively religious: either the Archbishop's comments are distinctive or they are not.) The strength of this objection is assessed in two ways. First, the report examines the significance of his contributions by assessing the extent to which they influenced broader political debate and were reported in the mainstream media. Second, it assesses the degree to which the Archbishop's participation in politics was distinctive, particularly as a consequence of its religious character.

The question that this report sets out to answer, then, is whether the role played by the Archbishop of Canterbury within English politics over the last thirty years is best understood as a valuable moral voice that has contributed to the national (and even global) common good, or as a series of self-serving, outdated, unrepresentative, unnecessary, or irrelevant contributions.

chapter 1 references

1. Kenneth Medhurst and George Moyser, *Church and Politics in a Secular Age* (Oxford: Clarendon, 1988), p. 5.

2. For further discussion see Grace Davie, *Religion in Modern Europe: A Memory Mutates* (Oxford: Oxford University Press, 2000), pp. 71-81.

3. See Appendix 1.

4. Paul Christopher Manuel & Margaret MacLeish Mott, "The Latin European Church: 'Une Messe Est Possible,'" in *The Catholic Church and the Nation-State: Comparative Perspectives*, ed. Paul Christopher Manuel, Lawrence C. Reardon and Clyde Wilcox (Washington DC: Georgetown University Press, 2006), p. 66.

5. "The Archbishops of Canterbury and York Issue Joint Open Letter", news release, 25 May 2001, releases/010525.htm.

6. Judith Judd, "Runcie Votes to Challenge the Law," 12 June 1983, *The Observer*.

7. See Humphrey Carpenter, *Robert Runcie: The Reluctant Archbishop* (London: Hodder & Stoughton, 1996).

8. See George Carey, *Know the Truth: A Memoir* (London: HarperCollins, 2004).

9. See Rupert Shortt, *Rowan's Rule: The Biography of the Archbishop of Canterbury* (London: Hodder & Stoughton, 2009); on his lapsed Labour Party membership, see Christopher Morgan, "Beware, Christian Soldier On Warpath," 2 February 2003, News Review 5, *The Sunday Times*.

10. Robert Runcie, speech to the Coningsby Club, London, 24 October 1984, "Church and State," in *One Light for One World* (London: SPCK, 1988), p. 142.

11. George Carey, Barnett Lecture, London, 5 October 1992, "Trust in the People: Democracy and the Christian Faith," in *Sharing A Vision* (London: Darton, Longman & Todd, 1993), p. 73.

12. Rowan Williams, speech at Westminster Abbey, London, 18 March 2008, "Archbishop's Holy Week Lecture: Faith and Politics," http://www.archbishopofcanterbury.org/1711.

13. Perhaps the only example relating to recent history is an unpublished doctoral thesis by Bruce Stephen Bennett, "The Archbishop of Canterbury in Politics, 1919-1939: Selected Case Studies" (PhD diss., University of Cambridge, 1992).

14. See George Moyser, *Church and Politics Today: Essays on the Role of the Church of England in Contemporary Politics* (Edinburgh: T&T Clark, 1985); Medhurst and Moyser, *Church and Politics*; Kenneth Medhurst and George Moyser, "The Church of England and Politics: The Politics of Establishment," *Parliamentary Affairs* 42:2 (1989): pp. 230-249; Kenneth Medhurst, "Reflections on the Church of England and Politics at a Moment of Transition," *Parliamentary Affairs*, 44:2 (1991): pp. 240-261; Kenneth Medhurst, "The Church of England: A Progress Report," *Parliamentary Affairs* 52:2 (1999): pp. 275-290; Henry B. Clark, *The Church Under Thatcher* (London: SPCK, 1993); Andrew Partington, *Church and State: The Contribution of the Church of England Bishops to the House of Lords During the Thatcher Years* (Bletchley: Paternoster, 2006); Andrew Partington and Paul Bickley, *Coming Off the Bench: The Past, Present and Future of Religious Representation in the House of Lords* (London: Theos, 2007).

15. George Carey, interview with author.

16. George Carey, speech at Lambeth Palace, 23 April 2002, "Holding Together: Church and Nation in the Twenty-First Century," http://web.archive.org/web/20021012173214/www.archbishopofcanterbury.org/speeches/020423.htm.

17. Carey, Barnett Lecture, 5 October 1992, p. 84.

18. Ibid., pp. 82-83.

19. Runcie, speech to Coningsby Club, 24 October 1984, pp. 142.

20. Robert Runcie, speech at Kent University, 20 February 1981, "Church and Society," in *Windows onto God* (London: SPCK, 1983), p. 73.

21. Runcie, speech to Coningsby Club, 24 October 1984, pp. 144-146.

22. Alan Rusbridger, "Interview with Rowan Williams," 21 March 2006, *The Guardian* website, http://www.guardian.co.uk/world/2006/mar/21/religion.uk.

23. "Archbishop Issues Letter to Party Leaders," news release, 31 March 2005, http://www.archbishopofcanterbury.org/869.

24. Stathis N. Kalyvas, *The Rise of Christian Democracy in Europe* (New York: Cornell University Press, 1996); Anthony Gill, *Rendering unto Caesar: The Catholic Church and the State in Latin America* (Chicago: University of Chicago Press, 1998); Carolyn M. Warner, *Confessions of an Interest Group: The Catholic Church and Political Parties in Europe* (Princeton: Princeton University Press, 2000); Anthony Gill, *The Political Origins of Religious Liberty* (Cambridge: Cambridge University Press, 2008).

25. "Archbishop's Defence of Faith Schools 'Disingenuous and Self-Serving'," National Secular Society, 13 March 2006, http://www.secularism.org.uk/archbishopsdefenceoffaithschools.html.

26. Terry Sanderson, "New Year's Message to the Archbishop of Canterbury," National Secular Society, 31 December 2003, http://www.secularism.org.uk/32706.html.

27. "Academies Bill – Secularist Arguments Rebuffed," National Secular Society, 23 July 2010, http://www.secularism.org.uk/academies-bill-secularist-argume.html.

28. Paper for the House of Lords consultation, National Secular Society, 1 December 2003, http://www.secularism.org.uk/uploads/lordsreform002.pdf, p. 10.

29. Response to Ministry of Justice, British Humanist Association, 17 November 2008, http://www.humanism.org.uk/filegrab/?f=BHA-Response-to-MoJ-consultation-%27An-Elected-Second-Chamber%27.pdf&ref=4367.

30. Anthony Gill, "Religion and Comparative Politics," *Annual Review of Political Science* 4 (June 2001): p. 131.

31. Peter Brierley, ed., *UKCH: Religious Trends No. 6, 2006/2007: Analyses from the 2005 English Church Census* (London: Christian Research, 2006), 12.2.

32. "Church and State," National Secular Society, paper presented to the UCL Constitution Unit Church and State Seminar, Limehouse, 11-12 July 2006, http://www.secularism.org.uk/uploads/churchandstate.pdf, p. 23.

33. Terry Sanderson, "Rowan Williams Declares War on Secularism," National Secular Society, 21 September 2007, http://www.secularism.org.uk/rowanwilliamsdeclareswaronsecula.html.

34. "Archbishop's Address Highlights the Need for Disestablishment," British Humanist Association, 10 February 2010, http://www.humanism.org.uk/news/view/482.

35. Polly Toynbee, "Homophobia, Not Injustice, is What Really Fires the Faiths," 9 January 2007, *The Guardian*, http://www.guardian.co.uk/commentisfree/2007/jan/09/comment.politics1.

36. Johann Hari, "Get Bishops Out of Our Law-Making," 18 February 2011, *The Independent*, http://www.independent.co.uk/opinion/commentators/johann-hari/johann-hari-get-bishops-out-of-our-lawmaking-2218130.html.

37. House of Lords consultation, National Secular Society, p. 3.

38. Terry Sanderson, "Rowan Williams Declares War".

2

taking the moral high ground: archiepiscopal politics in practice

With the four theoretical perspectives on archiepiscopal politics in place, we can now evaluate each against empirical evidence of how the Archbishop actually engaged in politics. The aim is to establish whether the Archbishop succeeded in making a valuable moral input motivated by the common good, as he often claimed, or whether his contribution was marked or undermined by the three objections that were outlined in the previous chapter.

In this chapter, eight policy areas are considered in turn: urban poverty; asylum and immigration; criminal justice; British armed conflict; environment and climate change; traditional moral issues; children and education; and public policy relating to religion. Although these provide a representative overview of his political engagement – including a number of topics in which the criticisms are most likely to be plausible, such as traditional morality and religious policy – some areas are inevitably neglected. Perhaps the biggest casualty is international development policy, although it is mentioned in passing in the section on climate change. Likewise, significant interventions on the miners' strike in the mid-1980s and the global financial crisis in the late 2000s are not included. In addition to documenting how the Archbishop has participated in each area of political debate, the sections also feature additional evidence, including how the officeholders understood their activity, how it was reported in the mainstream media, and the extent to which it corresponded to public opinion at the time. On the basis of this evidence, it is possible to evaluate the plausibility of each of the four theoretical perspectives.

urban poverty

Without doubt, the most high-profile occasion on which the Archbishop engaged in politics during this period was his foray into the debate about urban poverty in the mid-1980s. Published in December 1985, *Faith in the City* was a detailed report into the challenges that faced England's Urban Priority Areas (UPAs), such as poverty, unemployment, crime, and the shortage of adequate housing.[1]

The report made a series of specific recommendations to both the Church and the government on a range of issues relating to urban life. In response to one of its recommendations, the Church established the Church Urban Fund, which today continues to allocate financial resources to projects that serve urban communities. Among the report's recommendations to the government were that certain welfare benefits should be made more generous and that the provision of public sector housing should be expanded.

The report is particularly significant for this study because the commission that authored it was established by and acted in the name of the Archbishop. It was interpreted by some – not entirely without justification – as having been a direct attack on Thatcher's economic policies. The report pointed out, for instance, that UPAs had received less funding from central government since the election of the Conservative government in 1979, and criticised the government's flagship policy that allowed Council tenants to buy their homes. In an implied criticism of comments made by Cabinet minister Norman Tebbit, it dismissed the claim that the unemployed could simply "get on their bikes" to find work.[2] As others have subsequently observed, *Faith in the City*'s strong support for government intervention put it at odds with the economic liberalism that underpinned many of Thatcher's reforms.[3]

Throughout the remainder of the period, the Archbishop continued to make interventions on urban deprivation a key plank of his political engagement. Short follow-up reports were published under the tenures of all three of the officeholders. In 1990, *Living Faith in the City* concluded despairingly that for many "the picture looks bleaker than it did in 1985".[4] A second progress report, *Staying in the City*, recorded in 1995 that the situation was "as bad if not worse than it was ten years ago".[5] The final report in this period on the topic, *Faithful Cities*, was published in 2006. Reflecting the changing conditions in England's urban areas, it gave greater prominence than had its predecessors to wealth inequality and urban regeneration, with less attention paid to unemployment and welfare provision.[6]

Although the commissions that published the latter two reports did not act in the name of the Archbishop, it is clear that he continued to be closely involved in the project, with *Faithful Cities* featuring an introduction by Williams. In addition to these initiatives, all three officeholders raised the political profile of urban deprivation through speeches in the Lords. In a debate about the inner cities in 1987, Runcie called on the government to allocate greater resources to the poor,[7] while Carey delivered a similar message in his maiden speech to the Lords in 1991.[8] Shortly prior to the publication of *Faithful Cities*, Williams initiated a Lords debate about the contribution made by faith groups to urban communities.[9]

The publication of the original report provoked a major political debate about England's inner city areas. Before it had been published, an unnamed Conservative minister labelled it as "pure Marxist theology", thus securing for the Church front-page headlines.[10] Others soon followed suit, including one Conservative MP who dismissed the Anglican hierarchy as a "load of Communist clerics".[11] Media reaction to the report was predictably divided. An editorial for *The Times* delivered an unfavourable verdict on the "highly politicized report", largely because of its perceived opposition to free-market economic policies.[12] In another article for the newspaper, Digby Anderson of the Social Affairs Unit criticised the report's "one-sidedness".[13] Another right-leaning paper, the *Daily Mail*, criticised the report's apparent partisanship, remarking, "[i]t is the word of God which the Church of England should be bringing to our God-forsaken inner cities not soggy chunks of stale politics that read as if they have been scavenged from the Socialist Party's dustbin."[14] By contrast, an editorial in the left-leaning *Guardian* branded the government's reaction as "simply hypocritical".[15]

> *"It is the word of God which the Church of England should be bringing to our God-forsaken inner cities not soggy chunks of stale politics that read as if they have been scavenged from the Socialist Party's dustbin."*

Within days of its publication, dozens of opposition MPs had signed an Early Day Motion in the Commons that regretted the government's resort to "petty abuse and insults", while a handful of Conservative MPs backed an amended version of the EDM that "deplore[d]" the report.[16] By the time Runcie spoke at the General Synod about *Faith in the City* in February 1986 – two months after it was published – he was able to claim rightly that the Church had "generated a national debate", and that the report was already in its second printing having sold over 10,000 copies.[17]

The subsequent reports also stimulated some political debate, although they proved less controversial than the original document. In response to the publication of *Living Faith in the City* in 1990, an editorial for *The Times* remarked that "the Church has learnt a good lesson", although it nevertheless objected to some of the report's criticisms of government policy.[18] Whereas *The Times'* news article focused on the report's conciliatory tone towards the government,[19] *The Guardian's* equivalent piece emphasised the renewal of the Church's criticism of government policy.[20] The release of *Staying in the City* in 1995 was briefly reported in *The Times*,[21] but it appears to have been greeted with disappointment by some on the left, with Madeleine Bunting reporting criticisms in *The Guardian* that it was "bland" and "non-commital, in marked contrast to *Faith in the City*".[22] *Faithful Cities* was also reported in both publications in 2006.[23] While *The Guardian* followed it up with an interview with Fran Beckett, the Chief Executive of the Church Urban Fund,[24] in an opinion piece for *The Times* Edward Lucas criticised the report's neglect of "the people who create wealth and jobs", concluding, "Britain's inner cities could do with more capital, and fewer reports".[25]

Given that the reports touched on so many social issues, it is difficult to gauge accurately the extent to which the Archbishop's activity reflected or contradicted public opinion. Although only a partial indication, it is helpful to consider two measures from the *British Social Attitudes* survey, both of which suggest that the Archbishop was broadly in line with the popular mood. The first is public support for higher taxation and government spending. Throughout this period, support for a reduction in government spending (and taxation) remained low, never rising above ten percent. The remainder of the population was split between those who favoured greater taxation and those who supported the status quo. When *Faith in the City* was published in 1985, opinion was divided relatively evenly between these two groups. However, opinion was already moving in a more statist direction, and by 1998 support for higher spending reached a highpoint of 63 percent, before dropping back to 39 percent in 2008. This suggests that, at least for the first half of the period, the Archbishop's stance was in line with public opinion, and may even be said to have been ahead of the public mood.

Faith in the City recommended that the earnings disregards for Unemployment Benefit[26] should be increased and that the government should extend certain benefits to those unemployed for more than one year. Although it is not possible to measure public opinion on these exact proposals, public opinion data are available about the level of unemployment benefits, and they tell a similar story to support for higher government spending. According to the *British Social Attitudes* survey, popular opinion was in 1985 broadly supportive of the report's call for higher welfare payments, with 44 percent believing that unemployment benefit was too low, compared to 34 percent who said it was too generous. The number who said it was too low continued to rise, so that by 1993 this ten-point gap had grown to 31 points, with 55 percent of the population believing that it was too low. Opinion then gradually reversed over the second half of the period so that, by 2008, just 21 percent thought it was too low compared to 61 percent who said it was too high. Once again, these figures suggest that the Archbishop was broadly in line with the direction of public opinion in the first half of the period. Although that opinion reversed in the second half of the period, it should be remembered that the final report, *Faithful Cities*, published in 2006, moved away from many of these concerns and towards newer challenges facing urban areas.

Despite the Archbishop being broadly in line with popular opinion, however, support for religious activism on these issues appears to have been divided. When asked in 1990 for the *European Values Study* whether they thought it "proper for churches to speak out" on unemployment – a prominent focus of the early reports – respondents were fairly evenly split, with a few more people disagreeing (49 percent) than agreeing (45 percent). On the basis of this evidence, it is possible to evaluate the four theoretical perspectives outlined in chapter one. The most plausible criticism is that the Archbishop may have been motivated by the Church's interests rather than by altruism. The fact that the reports received substantial media coverage and were broadly in line with the direction of public opinion raises the possibility that they were intended to attract new members to the Church. When Fran Beckett was interviewed by *The Guardian*, the interviewer suggested that *Faithful Cities* could have been "an attempt to attract bums back to pews" – a charge that she denied.[27] However, the goal of proselytising seems unlikely given the increasingly ecumenical and interfaith character of the commissions that authored the reports. The accusation also ignores the fact that *Faith in the City* made more recommendations to the Church than to the government and was, as Hugo Young commented in *The Guardian*, a "self-lacerating document".[28]

The National Secular Society greeted the news that *Faithful Cities* had been commissioned by suggesting that it would "turn out to be just another propaganda exercise aimed at extracting further money from the public purse."[29] There is, however, little evidence to support this claim, which in any case conspicuously ignores the fact that a key recommendation of *Faith in the City* to the Church – the establishment of the Church Urban Fund – was exceptionally expensive. According to Carey in 1994, the "vast majority" of its funds came from local church congregations rather than from external sources.[30] Moreover, these resources do not appear to have been primarily used to further the Church's interests. A 2008 survey of projects funded through the CUF asked them to specify how they aimed to influence the lives of their beneficiaries. Of the seven options available, sharing their faith ranked bottom with 19 percent strongly agreeing. Options that ranked higher included "[b]uilding confidences" (72 percent), "empowering and resourcing [people]" (69 percent), and "equipping them with new skills" (48 percent).[31] Indeed, in spite of these efforts, attendance at the Church's religious services in urban areas continued to decline, albeit at a slower rate than in rural areas.[32] If the Archbishop was motivated by the Church's interests, it is likely that he was left disappointed.

Given that institutional interests are relatively weak in explaining the Archbishop's engagement with this area of policy, it seems reasonable to assume that the officeholders were justified in claiming moral motivations. In a speech to the General Synod in 1986, Runcie emphasised the theological imperative for action, commenting that "[i]t is impossible to be a Christian without responding" to urban deprivation.[33] The Church's sense of its mission is also important. The 1985 report noted that the Church's status as a "national Church" gave it "a particular duty to act as the conscience of the nation",[34] and the reports also drew on the experiences of local parish priests serving deprived communities.

This moral explanation is also supported by the background to the initiative. Much of the early enthusiasm for the project came from the sense of genuine need, and in particular the inner-city disturbances of the early 1980s. In a Lords debate about the Brixton disorders, Runcie referred to the matter as "a grave moral issue", and insisted that the Church was "determined not to abandon the inner city and retreat to suburbia".[35] The first suggestion for an Archbishop's commission on the matter was made by Canon Eric James in 1981 in a letter to *The Times*, in which he referred to "places like Brixton",[36] and the idea was subsequently supported by a group of senior bishops who represented urban areas. It is also highly likely that the personal experiences of the officeholders informed their moral vision. Canon James claimed that Runcie was particularly shaped by his curacy in a poor community in Newcastle in the 1950s,[37] while Carey cited the influence of his own upbringing in East London.[38]

The value of this moral voice does not appear to be undermined by the other two objections. The criticism that is easiest to dismiss is that the Archbishop's intervention was irrelevant to mainstream political debate. On the contrary, *Faith in the City* – and, to a lesser extent, its successors – provoked widespread debate about urban poverty. Grace Davie, a leading sociologist of religion, is quite justified in observing that the 1985 report "achieved what the Labour Party had so conspicuously failed to do; that is, to push issues of deprivation – and in particular urban deprivation – to the top of the political agenda."[38]

The suggestion that the Archbishop's engagement was outdated requires a little more consideration. One of the main criticisms made of *Faith in the City* was that it relied on outdated economic solutions to England's social problems. In the words of a *Times* editorial, "[a]re the Archbishop and the Commission really sure that it would be good Christian policy for the government to try again the policies which are so largely responsible for the state of affairs they so rightly deplore?"[40] The Environment Secretary, Kenneth Baker, likewise called the report "negative and out of date".[41] Responding to similar claims, Hugo Young wrote in *The Guardian* that "the Archbishop [...] showed rather greater prescience than the Government".[42] What this makes clear is that judgements about policies being "outdated" are very often a matter of perspective. In any event, given the subsequent direction of public opinion, the case for the Archbishop's moral approach to urban poverty being outdated appears weak. By way of conclusion, it seems reasonable to judge that the Archbishop succeeded, in this area of debate, in sounding a moral voice in support of the common good.

asylum and immigration

Asylum and immigration policy is one of the few topics on which the Archbishop's political engagement focused on the legislative agenda in Parliament. Widespread ecclesiastical activism on this issue appears to have begun in the 1970s,[43] and the first major focus of the Archbishop's attention during this period was the British Nationality Bill in 1981, which sought to revise the eligibility of some people to become British citizens. Such was the level of clerical disquiet at the government's proposals that Runcie joked in a speech to the Lords that "there have been references to the enthusiastic amateurs of the cloth tripping over themselves as they rush to the barricades."[44] During the passage of the bill through the Lords, Runcie used his seat there to full effect. In two highly critical speeches, he referred to the legislation as "seriously defective"[45] and "a bad Bill",[46] claimed that provisions in it had provoked "insecurity and feeling of being unwanted", and warned that it risked creating "first and second-class citizens".[47] In addition to speaking in the Lords debates, Runcie cast four votes in opposition to the government on this bill[48] - around one quarter of the total he cast as Archbishop - including one on an amendment that he himself had tabled.[49]

Runcie's successors continued the Archbishop's stance in support of immigrants' rights. Carey publicly raised concerns on at least three occasions. Along with the Catholic Archbishop of Westminster, he wrote a letter to *The Times* in 1991 in which he criticised government proposals to significantly restrict the right of asylum seekers to appeal against a refusal,[50] although he does not appear to have used his Lords seat to challenge the legislation. He again championed asylum seekers' rights in 1996, when he voted for an amendment to the Asylum and Immigration Bill in the House of Lords,[51] and subsequently signed another joint letter with senior church leaders to *The Times* in opposition to aspects of the legislation.[52] Following the introduction of the Immigration and Asylum Bill by the newly-elected Labour government, Carey expressed concerns in a press release about some of its provisions relating to the detention of asylum seekers.[53]

Williams appears to have shown less activism on immigration legislation than his predecessors, but nevertheless took a similar stance. During a debate in the General Synod in 2004, he warned that the government's Asylum and Immigration Bill risked "gravely reduc[ing] and imperil[ling] the civil rights of those most at risk."[54] Williams used his Lords seat in 2006 to question a government spokesman about the adequacy of chaplaincy services and pastoral support in Immigration Detention Centres,[55] and in 2005 he raised concerns about the government's policy of removing failed asylum seekers to Zimbabwe.[56]

Considering that the Archbishop has intervened relatively consistently in support of immigrants' rights, it is perhaps surprising to find that he did so against the grain of popular opinion. Accurately assessing this is made difficult by the fact that the officeholders tended to intervene on specific policy details that were not measured by opinion polls. Even so, the available data suggest that the Archbishop was significantly out of step with the popular mood on this topic. The *British Social Attitudes* survey records public support, between 1983 and 1996, for people of various national origins settling in Britain. To take one example, it found that, although hostility to settlement by Indians and Pakistanis fell during the period (from 71 percent to 53 percent), over half the population continued to be opposed in 1996. By contrast, support for settlement by these groups remained low throughout the period, both beginning and ending the period on just two percent. The survey also includes measures relating to the assessment of immigration more broadly, which shows a very similar picture. When asked in 1995 about the number of immigrants, just four percent favoured higher immigration, compared to 63 percent who favoured lower immigration. By 2003, support for higher immigration had risen slightly to six percent, but support for lower immigration had also risen, to 71 percent.

These data are in line with poll evidence from elsewhere. Over this period, Ipsos MORI tracked responses to the statement, "There are too many immigrants in Britain." Although the methodology varied a little, the broad trend is indisputable. In 1989, when their records began, 63 percent agreed with the statement, with net agreement (the percentage that agreed, minus the percentage that disagreed) at 45 points. By 1999, the proportion that agreed had fallen to 55 percent, with net agreement down to 22 points. The figures then rose towards the end of the period, with two polls in 2007 reporting 68 percent agreeing with the statement, and net agreement at between 46 and 55 points.[57]

The Archbishop's comments relating specifically to asylum seekers seem, once again, to have been out of line with popular sentiments. When asked in 2001 whether Britain should take no more asylum seekers, opinion was evenly divided with 44 percent responding either way. Whilst this may seem fairly well-balanced, the implication is that almost half of the population believed that Britain should not provide refuge even to those who would be in serious danger in their own countries. In the same poll, a remarkable 74 percent agreed that refugees come to Britain because they regard it as a "soft touch", while 59 percent agreed that "[a] very large number of those seeking asylum are cheats".[58]

> **The Archbishop has intervened relatively consistently in support of immigrants' rights, against the grain of popular opinion.**

The Archbishop's contribution to this area of policy debate was frequently reported by the national media.[59] The day after it printed Carey's joint letter with the Catholic Archbishop of Westminster about the Asylum Bill in November 1991, for instance, an editorial article in *The Times* implied that, although the government "was right" that asylum rules "need to be tightened", the Archbishops' letter also raised legitimate questions.[60] Shortly before his enthronement, Williams found himself at the centre of a minor media storm when he appeared to suggest in an interview for *The Sunday Times* that it would be reasonable to lock those with pending asylum claims in secure detention centres.[61] An article in *The Daily Express* responded positively to his comments,[62] whereas a piece in *The Guardian* noted that they were "in direct contradiction to much church opinion" and that they had been welcomed by the political right.[63]

In reality, it seems likely that his remarks were taken out of context. Indeed, the *Daily Mail* reported a clarification from Williams' spokesman that "he was not actually calling for" detention of asylum seekers, but was rather acknowledging the legitimacy of having the debate.[64]

Considering that the Archbishop's activity consistently contradicted public opinion, it seems unlikely that he was motivated by the Church's institutional interests. Indeed, had the Archbishop wanted to appeal to the population, there are good reasons to believe that taking a tougher stance on immigration would have been an attractive option. Responding in *The Daily Express* to Williams' apparent support for detention centres, Patrick O'Flynn suggested that "what he has said will greatly enhance the chances of the Church of England reconnecting with ordinary people."[65] Since retiring as Archbishop, Carey has on a number of occasions voiced concern about immigration, which have been regularly reported in the right-of-centre media.[66] The response of Max Hastings, writing for the *Daily Mail*, is particularly telling: "Amen, most of his listeners will have muttered, after themselves sounding the same alarm for years." He went on to suggest that Carey had not taken this stance whilst Archbishop because "Churchmen want to be seen to adopt 'Christian' attitudes."[67]

The influence of institutional interests is further undermined by the observation that immigration appears to be eroding the Church's dominance of England's religious 'sector'. Research in 2009 by IPPR found that around a quarter of Britain's immigrant population that claimed a religious affiliation was Muslim, while the fastest-growing Christian groups were Polish Catholics and African Pentecostals.[68] This evidence is supported by other research, which indicates that the growth in Pentecostalism in England is closely linked to immigration.[69] Following Williams' apparent support for the detention of asylum seekers, *The Guardian* printed two letters that implied that he may have been influenced by the Church's interests. One questioned whether the Archbishop would "be so persuaded of the merits of 'secure accommodation' for asylum seekers if they were members of the Church of England", while the other noted that asylum claimants "at the moment are inclined to be non-Christian and black".[70] Although, in reality, it is probable that Williams had not intended to take this stance, the two letters made a valid observation: had the Archbishop been motivated by the Church's institutional interests, there are good reasons to expect that he would have opposed immigration. The fact that this is the opposite of what happened is a powerful indicator that the Church's interests did not drive the Archbishop's activity on this topic.

The main alternative is that the Archbishop was motivated by a moral concern for the common good. This was the claim of Runcie, who commented in the Lords about the British Nationality Bill that "[i]t is because this Bill will give a shape and character to our future society that it is of such importance for us all."[71] This moral explanation is made more plausible by the fact that the officeholders seemed to be acting on pastoral concerns. All three officeholders were reported by the press as supporting particular immigration cases,[72] while both Carey and Williams released press statements about immigration policy after visiting immigration detention centres.[73] In one of his Lords speeches, Runcie quoted at length the experiences of a clergyman serving in East London and recounted a meeting he had attended with the Home Secretary and seven Brixton church leaders.[74] Elsewhere, Williams referred to the experiences of Anglican clergy operating in immigration detention centres.[75] These pastoral concerns appear to have been informed by their Christian moral values. For instance, Carey's joint letter with the Catholic Archbishop of Westminster in 1991 noted that, "[i]n signing the 1951 convention on the status of refugees, this country accepted the moral responsibility, which is also a Christian duty, of welcoming the true asylum seeker who knocks on our door".[76]

The most plausible of the three objections to the Archbishop's intervention in this area is that it was unrepresentative. Popular opinion throughout this period was firmly hostile to immigration, in contrast to almost all archiepiscopal political activity. This, however, does not so much constitute an objection to the Archbishop's intervention as an objection to the objection itself. If political interventions needed to be 'representative' in order to be legitimate, it would greatly impoverish national political debate.

The remaining objection is that the Archbishop's contribution was irrelevant to mainstream political debate. While it is certainly true that the Archbishop was not as central to the immigration debate as he was on urban poverty, it is also true that Runcie was clearly a significant player in the debate over the British Nationality Bill, using his seat in the Lords to vote, speak and table an amendment on the legislation. Although his successors did not agitate on this issue to the same degree, the fact that the media continued to report on their activity indicates that they were regarded as making an important contribution to this area of political debate. Indeed, the fact that the Archbishop generally acted in opposition to the overwhelming popular sentiment, apparently on the basis of theological and moral principles, may actually strengthen the case that his contribution added something distinctive to the political debate. Taken as a whole, it may be concluded that the Archbishop did indeed make a valuable contribution motivated by moral principles, although one that was nevertheless unrepresentative of public opinion.

criminal justice

In contrast to immigration policy, the Archbishop's contribution to debate about criminal justice during this period did not focus specifically on the parliamentary legislative agenda. The Archbishop's most significant contribution to this policy area was through a number of major lectures to the Prison Reform Trust, a charity that lobbies for a greater use of alternatives to prison and the improvement of prisoner conditions. The three officeholders each drew attention in their lectures to deficiencies in the existing prison system, including overcrowding and high rates of reoffending upon release, and argued that there should be greater use of restorative or community forms of justice.[77]

In addition to these major lectures, the Archbishop took a number of other opportunities to influence this area of policy. In 1983, Runcie initiated a debate in the House of Lords about violent crime, in which he made a number of suggestions, including that there be greater use of non-custodial sentences.[78] Williams used his Lords seat to highlight this area of policy on two occasions. In 2004, he initiated a debate about sentencing in which he called for greater emphasis on "restoration, reparation and rehabilitation",[79] and, in 2008, questioned a government spokesperson about the treatment of young offenders.[80] When the reintroduction of the death penalty was suggested in the early 1980s, Runcie publicly opposed the move.[81] He also contributed a foreword to a 1986 book based on the work of the British Council of Churches' Penal Group,[83] and the following year delivered a speech to the National Association of Victim Support Schemes in which he described imprisonment in Britain as "nasty, brutish and long".[83] In 1995, Carey was widely reported as criticising the news that the prison population had reached a record high.[84] Williams likewise made speeches about penal policy, including to the Church's General Synod[85] and at Worcester Cathedral.[86]

> *Christian morality is based on love rather than fear, upon grace rather than retribution.*

It is possible to discern a number of ways in which the Archbishop made a moral contribution to this area of policy. As might be expected, the officeholders articulated a moral disapproval of crime itself. Runcie, for instance, suggested that the causes of crime are "not just social and environmental" but "also moral and spiritual".[87] Carey likewise contended that "a moral community with an idea of goodness and evil" must have some "mechanism for naming and denouncing crimes".[88] Accordingly, both Runcie and Carey suggested that one method of reducing crime would be to foster strong moral values through families and schools.[89]

Perhaps more significantly, however, the Archbishop extended his moral assessment to the justice system itself. Indeed, Runcie suggested in his lecture to the Prison Reform Trust that "the way a society treats its offenders" is a good "indicator of the wider values which that society holds."[90] Drawing on Christian values in the same lecture, he claimed that it is impermissible to "blu[r] the distinction between revenge and justice",[91] and that "Christian morality is based on love rather than fear, upon grace rather than retribution."[92] When responding to calls to reintroduce the death penalty, Runcie sympathetically quoted a statement by the British Council of Churches that "[t]he judicial taking of life as a penalty for murder does not enhance the sacredness of human life but further devalues it."[93] In a similar way, Carey's lecture noted that a feature of the Judeo-Christian tradition is to "curb the instincts of revenge and replace them by justice linked to purposes of reconciliation and peace."[94]

The Archbishop's moral contribution is perhaps most evident in his emphasis of the human dignity and worth of individual prisoners. For instance, Runcie criticised prison conditions as failing to fully respect the "humanity" of prisoners,[95] and stressed that the Christian faith "combines a realism about the fundamental corruption of human nature with a determination not to despair about the potential in everyone for redemption."[96] Carey reflected this in his lecture to the Trust, in which he said, "as a Christian I cannot accept that people are irredeemable. Hope survives where faith and love are present."[97] Likewise, drawing on the words of wartime Archbishop William Temple, Williams observed that "a prisoner is never simply a prisoner".[98]

In contrast to such sentiments, public opinion was generally supportive of tough punishments for offenders throughout this period. Despite Runcie's opposition to capital punishment, poll data from Ipsos MORI report consistently high levels of support among the population at large.[99] Data from the *British Social Attitudes* survey report a high degree of support for tough measures in other areas of the justice system. In 1991, 67 percent agreed that stiffer sentences would be effective in cutting crime, which rose slightly to 70 percent in 1996. By contrast, sending fewer people to prison was regarded as ineffective by 65 percent in 1991 and by 76 percent in 1996. There was strong support for the suggestion that too many criminals are given too lenient punishments, with 79 percent agreeing in 1991, and 86 percent in 1996. Likewise, the suggestion that British courts give sentences that are too harsh was very unpopular, registering 70 percent disagreement in 1991. The proportion that agreed that prisoners have "much too easy a time" was also relatively high, at 64 percent in 1994 and 61 percent in 1996. In 1981, *The European Values Study* asked British people to choose from four options for what the main goal of imprisonment should be. The option that was closest to restorative justice – educating the prisoner – ranked as the third most popular choice (25 percent), behind making people pay for their wrongdoing (30 percent) and protecting other citizens (26 percent).

Despite popular support for tough penalties for crime, some pieces of data partially contradict this message. When asked in 2004 to select the two or three measures that would be most effective in cutting crime, just 11 percent chose imprisoning more offenders, compared to 57 percent who supported better parenting and 46 percent who called for better school discipline.[100] This appears to be in line with the call by Runcie and Carey for families and schools to teach moral values. According to *British Social Attitudes* data, opinion was split on whether prisons contain too many people who should have received a lighter punishment: in 1990, 48 percent agreed and 23 percent disagreed whereas, in 1994, 28 percent agreed and 40 percent disagreed. Likewise, just 36 percent thought in 1991 that sending more people to prison would be effective in reducing crime, although the figure did rise to 48 percent in 1996. In 1994, respondents were informed that "[t]here are a number of ways of dealing with criminals who are not a big threat to society", before being asked their opinion on a range of these options. Although the question may legitimately be criticised as being too leading, 73 percent supported community service as an alternative to prison, while 60 percent supported probation, and 64 percent training and counselling. On the whole, it seems fair to conclude that the Archbishop's support for better treatment of prisoners was broadly out of step with popular opinion, although it is likely that some of his specific proposals would have resonated with many people.

Although clearly not as newsworthy as in other policy areas, the Archbishop's comments about this area of policy were nevertheless reported in the national press. The three lectures to the Prison Reform Trust attracted particularly wide coverage.[101] Other interventions were also reported, including Runcie's Lords debate,[102] his speeches to the National Association of Victim Support Schemes,[103] his 1986 book foreword,[104] and Carey's criticism of police numbers.[105]

As might be expected, media comment was particularly scathing from right-of-centre publications. Following Carey's criticism of the government's "prison works" policies in 1995, the Home Secretary, Michael Howard, penned a relatively measured response for the *Daily Mail*.[106] The *Daily Mail* itself served up a less conciliatory piece: "It is the suffering of the criminals' victims, the number of offenders, and the laxness of jail discipline which should horrify Dr Carey and the nation. Not the fact that criminals are imprisoned."[107] When Carey delivered his speech to the Prison Reform Trust the following year, the publication's response was even more critical: "Unlike so many of his fellow citizens, the Archbishop of Canterbury lives his life comfortably free of crime and all its miserable consequences."[108] By contrast, a letter to *The Times* from a number of experts – including academics and former senior civil servants, as well as Runcie – praised Carey for "speaking with great moral authority and drawing on extensive pastoral experience of the prisons."[109]

At times, the officeholders explicitly claimed to be offering a moral perspective on this topic of debate. In his speech to the Prison Reform Trust, for instance, Runcie commented that the issue of penal reform had moved "towards the centre of our moral awareness".[110]

This explanation is supported by the fact that there are clear pastoral dimensions to this policy area. In common with urban poverty, it is likely that the presence of clergy in local communities gave the officeholders a better awareness of the social costs of crime. In his speech to the Prison Reform Trust, for instance, Carey referred to his own experience as a prison chaplain in the 1970s,[111] while in his speech to the General Synod Williams referred to the work performed in prisons by local congregations and Christian charities.[112]

By contrast, it appears most unlikely that the Archbishop was motivated by the Church's interests. Apart from its prison chaplaincy work, the Church does not appear to have had institutional interests directly at stake. The fact that the Archbishop's broad stances were significantly out of line with public opinion also casts doubt on this suggestion. It therefore seems fair to conclude that moral concerns provide a much better explanation of the Archbishop's behaviour than do institutional interests.

The other two criticisms, however, are a little more compelling. Whilst it is unreasonable to argue that the Archbishop's comments were outdated, it is certainly true that they were unrepresentative of popular opinion. There is also some evidence to support the claim that the Archbishop's moral input was unnecessary, as it replicated the contribution of other participants in political debate. Indeed, the very existence of the Prison Reform Trust, which has published literature by a range of other speakers, proves that the Archbishop was not alone in making these arguments. Nevertheless, the fact that the Trust chose to invite all three officeholders to deliver its lectures suggests, at the very least, that they regarded the primate as effective in highlighting their cause. The fact that the press chose to report a significant number of the Archbishop's interventions on this topic indicates that journalists also regarded his contribution as being sufficiently important to justify attention. Moreover, although other individuals and organisations were making similar arguments, it is especially noteworthy that the Archbishop promoted this cause often by drawing explicitly on Christian theological and moral arguments. In this way, his contribution was distinctive even if others argued for similar policy outcomes. Overall, it seems reasonable to conclude that the Archbishop's input into political debate about criminal justice issues represents a moral voice in support of the common good, albeit one that partially replicated other voices and that was unrepresentative of British popular opinion.

British armed conflict

In chapter one it was suggested that the Archbishop's political role encompasses both participation in political debate and giving meaning to the more 'sacred' moments of national life, such as mourning and death. These two strands come together, perhaps to a greater extent than in any other area of policy, in debates about armed conflict. In his study into the political debates that accompanied British armed conflict over the past two centuries, Philip Towle observes the tendency for the British government to justify warfare on moral grounds rather than on national interest, and this may have made the Church particularly prominent in these debates.[113] This section of the report focuses on four major conflicts: the Falklands war (1982), the Gulf war (1991), the Afghanistan war (2001-), and the Iraq war (2003-09).

The first major military operation during this period was the Falklands war, which was launched in response to Argentina's invasion of Britain's Falkland Islands in 1982. Runcie strongly supported Britain's military retaliation, including in two speeches to the House of Lords.[114] At the subsequent thanksgiving service, however, he attracted the fury of some government ministers for the tone of his sermon, in which he remembered "the relations of the young Argentinian soldiers who were killed".[115] John Nott, then Defence Secretary, scathingly refers to "the stupidity of the bishops" in his autobiography.[116]

The second episode of armed conflict was the Gulf war, which was launched in 1991 during the final weeks of Runcie's archiepiscopate. Once again, Runcie supported the government's stance, including in two speeches in the Lords,[117] and in private conversations with the Prime Minister, John Major.[118] The third war was the invasion of Afghanistan in 2001, launched in response to the terrorist attacks on New York. Although Carey does not seem to have been especially prominent in the political debate, he was reported as describing it as "a necessary conflict".[119]

The final major conflict during this period was the 2003 invasion of Iraq, which was also the only conflict of the four that the Archbishop unequivocally opposed. When the prospect of war was first raised, Carey voiced his concerns in private with the government, including in a letter to Tony Blair[120] and in a meeting with the Cabinet minister Robin Cook.[121] As war became more likely, Carey became more vocal in his opposition, and took the opportunity of his final Sunday as Archbishop to warn against military action.[122] The Archbishop's opposition to the Iraq war continued when Williams assumed the role late in 2002. Shortly before war was declared, Williams raised his concerns in a private meeting with Tony Blair at 10 Downing Street.[123] He also released a joint statement with the Catholic Archbishop of Westminster in which they urged continued engagement through the United Nations and appeared to question "the moral legitimacy" of declaring war.[124]

In addition to assessing the moral case for engaging in specific conflicts, the Archbishop also raised moral questions about the conduct of war. As might be expected, the officeholders called for the number of human casualties to be minimised. Despite supporting the Falklands war, for instance, Runcie wrote an article for *The Times* in 1982 in which he argued that the escalation of casualties may make it necessary to reassess Britain's response.[125] Similarly, Williams' joint statement with other religious leaders at the start of the Iraq conflict drew attention to "[t]he rights and needs of civilians" in the country.[126] A second theme was to warn against nationalistic triumphalism. In relation to the Gulf war, Runcie quoted the Christian theologian Dietrich Bonhoeffer to remind members of the House of Lords that "God is [...] not on any side".[127] The clearest expression of this concern is probably found in Runcie's sermon at the Falklands thanksgiving service.

A third significant strand of his contribution was to identify and highlight the potential negative consequences of conflict for religious communities. Prior to the Falklands war, Runcie emphasised in the Lords that the predominantly Catholic Argentina was "a Christian people",[128] and in the run-up to the Gulf war warned that carelessly associating Iraq with Islam could have negative consequences for Britain's small Muslim community.[129] When Britain invaded Afghanistan in 2001, Carey emphasised that the action should not be interpreted as a war between two rival religions.[130] Williams' joint statement with religious leaders before the Iraq war pledged "to resist any attempt to drive our communities apart".[131] This particular sensitivity to the implications of armed conflict for religious communities may reasonably be regarded as one of the Archbishop's most valuable contributions to this topic of debate.

There is convincing evidence that the Archbishop's engagement with this area of policy was deeply influenced by moral and theological reflection. In particular, the officeholders drew on just war theory, which has informed the Christian church's response to armed conflict for centuries. In a helpful introduction to the topic, Richard Harries (who was the Bishop of Oxford between 1987 and 2006) sets out five criteria for justifiably participating in war. On the basis of these criteria, he argues that military action was justifiable in the Falklands, Gulf and Afghanistan, but not in the case of Iraq.[133] There is strong evidence that Harries influenced the officeholders' thinking about this area of policy during this period,[133] and the conclusions reached in his article clearly correspond to the actual stances taken by the Archbishop.

Statements by the officeholders appear to corroborate this analysis. Both Runcie and Williams delivered lectures to the Royal Institute of International Affairs in which they reflected on just war theory.[134] Significantly, the argument advanced in Williams' lecture was that the 2003 invasion of Iraq failed to satisfy its requirements. When commenting on individual conflicts, Runcie referred to both the Falklands and Gulf wars as "just".[135] Although Carey expressed reservations about just war theory, it seems clear that his stances were nevertheless informed by its considerations. On the Gulf war, for instance, he said: "I have always questioned the just war theory and I question the medieval basis of it. But I believe that certain wars are justifiable, even if not entirely just."[136] He made similar comments in relation to the Afghanistan war.[137] Despite his reluctance to sign up fully to just war thinking, Carey nevertheless confirmed that he and other bishops "had many a debate on the just war and what constitutes a just war".[138]

Public opinion about each of the four major conflicts seems to have been broadly in line with the Archbishop's stance. According to poll data from Ipsos MORI, public satisfaction with the government's handling of the situation in the Falklands remained high throughout the conflict and grew steadily from 60 percent in April 1982 to 84 percent shortly after hostilities ceased in June.[139] Support for the Gulf war similarly rose steadily from 80 percent in the first week of the conflict to 88 percent in week seven.[140] Following the 2001 terrorist attacks in New York, Ipsos MORI recorded that British support for military action against Afghanistan stood at 74 percent. Although support dropped slightly to 66-69 percent by November 2001, it is clear that popular approval remained very high when the decision was taken for British forces to participate.[141] By contrast, the British people were much less enthusiastic about war in Iraq. According to poll data from Ipsos MORI, public approval of Tony Blair's handling of the situation stood at just 26 percent in January 2003, against 62 percent that disapproved. Although approval rose to 36 percent at the beginning of March, it is clear that public support for the Iraq war was markedly lower than for the three other major conflicts during the period.[142]

The Archbishop's activity in this area of political debate was widely reported by the media, particularly in the case of Iraq. Indeed, three journalists writing for the *Guardian* shortly

> **"The Prime Minister has every right to be furious at Runcie's wet and woolly approach."**

before the Iraq war began were probably justified in claiming that "opposition to the war on Iraq has given [the Church] its highest public profile on a secular, political issue for nearly 20 years, since its tussles with the Thatcher government over social policy."[143] Several weeks later, an editorial in the same newspaper underscored the political significance of Williams' joint statement with his Catholic counterpart about the possibility of war. It noted that "the churches are at the centre of opposition and concern about the probable coming conflict", and claimed that, by releasing the statement, "[t]he archbishops have greatly increased the pressures on Mr Blair".[144]

Understandably, journalistic comment was particularly forthcoming on the two occasions that the Archbishop clashed with the government: Runcie's sermon at the Falklands thanksgiving service, and the 2003 invasion of Iraq. Commenting on the Falklands service, the *Sun* stated that "[t]he Prime Minister has every right to be furious at [Runcie's] wet and woolly approach", and added, "[b]ut if the Archbishop – and sadly other Church leaders – are so clearly out of tune with the vast majority of their fellow countrymen, is it any wonder that so few go to church nowadays?"[145] The *Daily Mail* featured the story as its front page headline, and commented inside, "If there is to be a Church *of* England, surely on such an occasion above all others, it should be *with* England!"[146]

As might be expected, Williams' opposition to the Iraq war attracted both praise and criticism. Melanie Phillips complained in the *Daily Mail* about the Archbishop's unwillingness to oppose the evil of Saddam Hussein's regime, adding "[t]he churches, along with the others who are against this war, have lost their moral way."[147] An editorial in the *Daily Telegraph* made the calmer objection that, although church leaders were justified in "reminding us of general Christian principles, neither [the Archbishop of Canterbury nor the Catholic Archbishop of Westminster] is qualified to enter into a detailed discussion of whether the removal of Saddam Hussein will lead to more or less violence in the world."[148] A more positive assessment was made by Donald Macintyre, writing for the *Independent*, who questioned "whether a fresh UN mandate would be morally desirable, let alone necessary in international law, as the impressive new Archbishop of Canterbury [...] persuasively maintains."[149] Williams' stance on Iraq may even have earned him support from some unlikely quarters. In an article for the *Guardian's* website in 2007, Stephen Bates reflected, "[i]f only the prime minister had listened on the one issue the Archbishop of Canterbury got right: the invasion of Iraq."[150]

Of the three objections, the one that the Archbishop is least vulnerable to is that his contributions were outdated or unrepresentative. On the contrary, in his general stances at least, he seems to have been perfectly aligned with the popular mood. Yet it also seems highly doubtful that this correlation resulted from a desire to enhance the Church's popularity, thereby furthering its institutional interests. Although it is certainly true that his stances towards the four major conflicts were broadly in line with popular opinion, key elements of his behaviour cannot be explained in this way. A particularly clear example is his consistent refusal to pander to nationalistic triumphalism, in spite of media and political pressure, most notably in the case of the Falklands thanksgiving service, when popular approval of the government's actions was at its height.

Because the Archbishop was aligned with public opinion, the objection that he is most vulnerable to is that his contribution was irrelevant or replicated the contributions of other commentators. To an extent, this criticism is justified: certainly, there was no shortage of anti-war spokesmen willing to fill column inches or to address anti-war rallies in early 2003. Nevertheless, the extensive media coverage of the Archbishop's comments, particularly in the case of Iraq, suggests that his contribution was newsworthy in its own right. His input to this area of political debate retained a distinctively Christian tone, in particular through Runcie's and Williams' use of just war theory. Moreover the Archbishop's

> "If only the prime minister had listened on the one issue the Archbishop of Canterbury got right: the invasion of Iraq."

position as the leader of the established Church led him to pay particular attention to the impact of war on religious communities, a perspective that was surely far less prominent in other contributions to political debate on armed conflict. It therefore seems fair to conclude that the Archbishop's contribution to this area of political debate, while in the same vein as public opinion, was not a slave to that opinion, and managed to retain a distinctive, and valuable, moral tone.

environment and climate change

Political attention to the environment and climate change markedly increased over the period studied in this report, and this trend is reflected in the behaviour of the Archbishop. Although Runcie had already made a number of passing comments about green issues,[151] his first major contribution came only in 1989 when he delivered a sermon at Canterbury Cathedral for the Festival of Faith and the Environment. In it, he argued that "humans are acting imprudently, polluting and squandering the riches of the earth at a pace which far exceeds the rate of natural renewal".[152]

Attention to environmental concerns continued to grow steadily under Carey's archiepiscopate. Shortly before his appointment as Archbishop, Carey endorsed Runcie's message in a speech to his local Green Party,[153] and early in his tenure he declared himself to be "a green archbishop".[154] His comment on this topic became particularly prominent around the turn of the century. In a lecture to mark the millennium, he warned of "the damage we are causing to nature",[155] while his 2001 New Year message warned that mankind's "energy-burning lifestyles are pushing our planet to the point of no return".[156] Later in 2001, he and the Archbishop of York identified "the task of caring responsibly for all of God's creation" as an important issue in the general election.[157]

The Archbishop's attention to environmental issues continued to intensify under Williams, and by the end of the period it was arguably one of his highest political priorities. Indeed, such was Williams' enthusiasm for the topic that in 2005 the Green Party endorsed him as being "on our political wavelength".[158] In 2004 he delivered his first major lecture on the topic, in which he urged the British government to show greater international leadership.[159] He also joined debates about the issue in specifically Christian forums, such as the Church's General Synod[160] and the World Council of Churches Assembly.[161] Williams continued Carey's efforts to raise environmental concerns in general elections, selecting it as one of four key issues in a letter to party leaders prior to the 2005 election,[162] and referring to it in an article for the *Church Times* in advance of the 2010 election, co-authored with the Archbishop of York.[163]

A substantial amount of Williams' activity focused on the international response to climate change. In advance of the 2007 UN Climate Change Conference in Bali, he signed a joint letter, along with his counterparts from Sweden and German, calling on European leaders to "secure the necessary framework agreement".[164] He also recorded a video message to religious leaders at the conference.[165]

The following year, he again signed a joint letter with his Swedish and German counterparts, urging Nicolas Sarkozy (at the time the French President and the President of the Council of the European Union) to push for progress on climate change at the European level.[166]

His activism in advance of the 2009 UN Climate Change Conference in Copenhagen included publishing a prayer for Environment Sunday,[167] convening a meeting of senior faith leaders issuing in a joint statement,[168] speaking at an ecumenical Environment Service in Westminster,[169] and travelling to deliver a sermon at Copenhagen Cathedral during the summit itself.[170]

Data from across the period suggest that the Archbishop was broadly in line with public opinion in his environmental interventions. Polls by Ipsos MORI during this period found that a large proportion of the population was concerned about climate change, although the figure dropped slightly from 82 percent in 2005 to 71 percent in 2010.[171]

There are also strong indications that the population supported the Archbishop's decision to publicly voice his priorities on this topic. The *European Values Study* records that, in 1990, 60 percent of the British population thought it appropriate for churches to speak out on ecological and environmental issues, compared to 34 percent that disagreed.

There also appears to have been strong popular support for political action on environmental issues. When asked in opinion polls who should be mainly responsible for tackling climate change, national governments came top in both 2005 (39 percent) and 2010 (32 percent), followed closely by the international community (32 percent in 2005, and 30 percent in 2010).[172]

There are also good indications that the population was supportive of the government taking tough action. According to data from the *British Social Attitudes* survey, 66 percent agreed in 1990 that the government should do more to protect the environment, even if it led to an increase in taxes, although the figure dropped slightly to 59 percent by 1997. Early in 2010, Ipsos MORI asked whether it was appropriate to spend taxpayers' money on British projects designed to tackle climate change. Despite being conducted at a time when there was broad political acceptance of the need for a reduction in public spending, 68 percent said they would probably or definitely vote in favour, compared to just 20 percent who indicated they would vote against.[173]

Press coverage in this area has been generally positive. Following Runcie's first foray into this terrain, an editorial in *The Times* noted that "the Church's espousal of these concerns can contribute powerfully to the material salvation of the planet from mankind's greed and indifference." However, it also argued that "the Church's main business" is to respond to "the spiritual salvation of man", adding that "[t]he Church has to remember that in terms of its own title deeds [the latter] remains the more important".[174]

Williams' political comments about environmental matters were frequently reported in the national press,[175] and he also gave a number of interviews to the broadcast media, including the BBC Radio 4 *Today* programme and BBC2's *Newsnight*.[176] Very often, the press comment on his statements was positive. For example, the environmental campaigner and future Conservative MP, Zac Goldsmith, opened one of his columns for *The Guardian* by quoting Williams.[177] Coverage has not been uniformly positive, however. In response to one of Williams' contributions to this area of debate, the *Daily Mail* published an article by Richard Littlejohn, which complained that "[h]e doesn't seem to have noticed that the world has managed to look after itself for the past few million years through plague, pestilence and Ice Age".[178]

Analysis of the Archbishop's contribution to this topic reveals attention to two significant moral dimensions of environmental activism. The first is the need for right relationship between humanity and creation. In his 1989 speech, Runcie remarked that creation "has an intrinsic value by no means reducible to its benefit to human beings",[179] while Carey observed in 2001 that "it was God's intention that humankind should serve and tend God's glorious creation".[180]

In an article for *The Guardian*, Williams made a similar point by writing about the Christian belief that "the world is God's before it is ours – never just a possession – and that we are in God's hands in life and death".[181]

Elsewhere, Williams observed that "the biblical picture presents us with a humanity that can never be itself without taking on the case and protection of the life of which it's a part." As such, he said, the decision about how to relate to creation is "a choice about how genuinely human we want to be".[181]

The second of the two moral dimensions is to be in right relationship with other human beings. In particular, the Archbishop sought to pay attention to the effects of climate change on the world's poorest people. Throughout this period, the Archbishop paid significant attention to the topic of international development more broadly. For instance, Runcie criticised the low priority given by the British government to global poverty,[183] while Carey addressed a London demonstration organised for the Jubilee 2000 campaign,[184] and Williams called on the government to push for international progress on achieving the Millennium Development Goals.[185] Carey connected international development issues with climate change in a 2001 speech in which he noted, among other developments, the expansion of the deserts into previously fertile agricultural land.[186]

Emphasis on this connection was maintained by Williams, who warned in a media interview that "millions, billions, of people" could die through starvation and flooding. He also extended his concern to include future generations, arguing that it is "a profoundly immoral policy and lifestyle that doesn't consider those people who don't happen to share the present moment with us".[187]

The claim that the officeholders were driven by moral concerns appears all the more compelling given that there does not appear to be any direct way in which the Archbishop's environmental activism furthered the Church's institutional interests. Of course, the fact that the Archbishop's comments were generally in line with public opinion does open the possibility that this area of debate was something of a PR exercise, intended to indirectly promote the Church's interests by enhancing its perceived social authority and popular appeal. Commenting on Runcie's 1989 sermon, an editorial in *The Times* drew attention to this objection. "Cynics will say has this merely proves that the Church has forgotten its own message, and will climb on any bandwagon that seems to be going somewhere."[188]

This explanation does seem somewhat doubtful, however, as there is precious little evidence to suggest that the Archbishop's prioritisation of this issue has done anything to rally church attendance figures. Given that the Archbishop was in line with public opinion, the suggestion that he articulated an outdated conception of morality is still less convincing.

The most plausible objection is that his input was unnecessary as it replicated the contributions of more authoritative and specialist figures. This objection was raised powerfully by Stephen Glover in the *Daily Mail*. "One of his pet subjects is global warming. There may be nothing wrong with that – except that there are already many people, some of them rather more expert than he is, lecturing us about its supposed perils."[189]

 It is undoubtedly true that none of the officeholders were trained scientists, and neither was there a shortage of political leaders willing to champion the cause. Yet this does not mean that explicitly moral contributions did not also make a valuable contribution to this area of debate. As the editorial in *The Times* put it after Runcie's 1989 sermon, "environmentalism is looking for an underlying rationale more noble than enlightened self-interest. There are spiritual as well as scientific resonances to be sounded."[190]

In fact, rather than merely replicating secular voices, the Archbishop's contribution took on a distinctively Christian character. As with the issue of armed conflict, the officeholders drew explicitly on theological and biblical arguments when making their case. Runcie's 1989 sermon, for instance, drew repeatedly on biblical passages, while Carey observed that "the Bible – from Genesis to Revelation – has a strong doctrine of environmental and ecological concern".[191]

In addition to theological beliefs, there is also evidence that the structure of the Church – as part of the global Anglican Communion – enhanced the value of the Archbishop's contribution. In an article for *The Guardian*, Williams reported comments made by the Anglican Bishop of Polynesia about the threat that rising ocean levels already presented to some islands in the Pacific.[192] The main objections to the Archbishop's role consequently appear particularly weak in this area of policy, and as such it seems fair to conclude that he made a valuable contribution in support of the common good.

traditional moral issues

In the five policy areas considered so far, the evidence suggests that the Archbishop made a valuable contribution to political debate, despite being partially vulnerable to some of the three objections. The remaining three sections look at policy areas on which the objections are expected to be most convincing. In this section, archiepiscopal engagement with two types of "traditional moral issue" is examined: sex and relationships, and the sanctity of life. The main charge that can be made against the Archbishop in these policy areas is that he was out of touch with the population. It is also theoretically possible that a religious organisation may decide to promote traditional morality in order to further its institutional interests, such as by enhancing its social authority and status.[193]

Of the three officeholders under discussion, the highest priority to issues sex and relationships was given by Carey. Towards the end of his tenure, for instance, he issued a series of statements in support of the newly-instituted National Marriage Week,[194] and made passing comment in a 2000 speech to the social cost, particularly to children, of "divorce rates and the undermining of marriage as an institution".[195]

He also participated in political debate about homosexuality, in large part because his archiepiscopate coincided with the election of a Labour government intent on social reform. Carey publicly expressed concern about the decision to lower the age of consent for gay men,[196] and when the Sexual Offences (Amendment) Bill came before the Lords in 1999 he voted for an amendment that was intended to effectively reject the change.[197] He later voiced his concerns about the government's intention to repeal Section 28, which outlawed the promotion of homosexuality in British schools.[198]

Although not quite as vocal as Carey on these matters, the other two officeholders also made comments on the topic. Runcie expressed concern about marriage failure, both in a speech to the General Synod[199] and in an article for *The Times*.[200] In 1985, the Archbishop apparently lobbied peers in support of the Marriage Bill, which was intended to relax restrictions on marriage between step-relations.[201] In 2007, Williams followed Carey's lead by speaking at the launch of National Marriage Week, arguing that marriage provides an "enhanced kind of human experience" and an "enlarged sense of what humanity is all about".[202] Two years later, at the launch of the *Good Childhood Report* in 2009, he stressed the social value of marriage. "[I]t will not serve us as a society, and it will not serve the growing generation, if we simply regard marriage as just one option in the marketplace of lifestyles."[203] In contrast to Carey, Williams is known to be personally sympathetic to the case for accepting committed same-sex sexual relationships.[204] Nevertheless, he publicly objected to the government's Sexual Orientation Regulations, to which we will turn later in this chapter.

> "I am very worried about the morality of simply sounding off"

Yet, despite the Archbishop's broadly conservative position, there are some surprising features to his contribution to this area of political debate. Runcie's speech to the Synod, which was mentioned above, urged the Church to not be "preoccupied with divorce".[205] In fact, his only Lords speech that dealt primarily with sexual matters was on a measure to allow divorcees to be ordained.[206] On that occasion, rather than the Archbishop being a conservative brake on the state, it was in fact the Commons that rejected the Church's more liberal policy. Even more unexpectedly, when the Lords considered the introduction of Section 28 in 1988, Runcie voted for an opposition amendment that aimed to dilute its effect.[207] Around the time of Williams' appointment, there was speculation that he would abandon Carey's more conservative stance on sexual issues.[208] In a subsequent interview, Williams refused to condemn cohabiting couples, later adding, "I am very worried about the morality of simply sounding off."[209] Even Carey, who was probably the most conservative on these issues, was a long way from being rigid or monomaniacal in his focus. Early in his tenure he confessed "a great impatience with those who become so fixated on the sins they see around them, especially sins of the flesh."[210] In the aftermath of the Conservative Party's "back to basics" campaign in support of family values in 1993, he delivered two notable speeches about marriage and the family. The first of them was interpreted by *The Guardian* as an attack on the Conservatives' rhetoric.[211] In the second he attacked "[c]onfident generalisations" about single parenthood, and commented that "'Back to the 1950s!' is not a message that will be listened to,"[212] which again could be interpreted as a critique of the Conservative government.

It seems fair to conclude that the Archbishop's political stance on sexual matters was generally, though not exclusively, conservative. Yet even this moderate conservatism was often out of kilter with popular opinion. According to the *British Social Attitudes* survey, towards the beginning of the period, in 1983, around 50 percent responded that same-sex sexual relationships are always wrong, compared to 17 percent that responded that they are never wrong. Opinion then liberalised steadily and, by 2007, 26 percent felt same-sex sexual relations are always wrong, compared to 39 percent who said they are never wrong. However, although the Archbishop was clearly swimming against the tide of liberalising attitudes, he was far from alone in his social conservatism. When Carey commented on gay issues in 2000, net opinion was still marginally conservative, with 37 percent regarding homosexual relationships as being always wrong and 34 percent responding that they are not at all wrong. A separate poll by Ipsos MORI for the *Daily Mail* found support for the retention of Section 28, and strong disapproval of the government's intention to lower the age of consent for gay men.[213]

In contrast to his comments on sex and relationships, it appears that Carey was almost entirely silent on sanctity of life issues. Runcie was also relatively quiet on this topic, although he did cast three Lords votes in support of legislation that sought to tighten the law on issues relating to abortion.[214] In a press interview towards the end of his archiepiscopate, Runcie indicated that his views on abortion had become more conservative over time.[215] Williams appears to have given greatest attention to these matters, although that may be because it was during his primacy that stem-cell research and euthanasia were at their most prominent as political issues. Following the publication of the Assisted Dying for the Terminally Ill Bill in January 2004, Williams wrote a joint letter with his Catholic counterpart to the appropriate Lords Select Committee, in which they outlined their opposition to the legislation.[216] When the bill was introduced again in November 2004, Williams responded in an article for *The Times* that it risked undermining the "sense of unconditional human worth and value".[217] Following the introduction of the bill again in November 2005, Williams opposed it by speaking and voting in the Lords.[218] He was also interviewed about the legislation on the BBC's *Today* Programme, and signed a joint letter to *The Times* with the Catholic Archbishop of Westminster and the Chief Rabbi.[219]

Similar levels of activism are evident with respect to the Human Fertilisation and Embryology Bill in 2008, which Williams opposed both in a Lords speech – warning about the movement "towards a more instrumental view of how we may treat human organisms"[220] – and through the media.[221] In the run-up to the 2005 general election, he entered an already active public debate about abortion by penning an article for *The Sunday Times*,[222] and two years later wrote a letter to *The Observer* to mark the fortieth anniversary of the Abortion Act.[223]

The population tended to be more liberal than the Archbishop with regard to abortion. It should be recognised that the available public opinion data do not provide a perfect point of reference, as during this period the Archbishop has not lobbied for abortion to be made illegal. Nevertheless, the figures do provide a good indication of public approval for abortion. Between 1980 and 2006, Ipsos MORI measured public opinion on whether "abortion should be made legally available for all who want it". Although no clear trend is evident, the proportion that agreed (54-64 percent) was consistently higher than that which disagreed (25-35 percent).[224] This is supported by data from the *British Social Attitudes* survey, which records opinion from across the period on the circumstances under which abortion should be legal. Throughout the period, it recorded overwhelming support for legalised abortion where the woman's life is seriously endangered, where the woman was raped, and where there is a strong chance of defect in the baby. In other cases, however, there is clear evidence of a shift in opinion. Between 1983 and 2008, for instance, the proportion that agreed that abortion should be legal where "[t]he woman decides on her own she does not wish to have the child" increased from 37 percent to 60 percent. Conversely, the proportion that disagreed fell steadily from 55 percent to 33 percent, reaching a low of 28 percent in 2007 when Williams marked the fortieth anniversary of the Abortion Act. During this period, opinion also appears to have been strongly supportive of legalised euthanasia. According to *British Social Attitudes* data from 1983 to 2005, between 75 and 83 percent agreed that doctors should be permitted to end the life of a patient with an incurable disease if the patient requested it.

When the two sets of issues – sexual relationships and sanctity of life – are taken together, some conclusions can be drawn about the Archbishop's attitude to traditional morality. Chapter one noted the claim of the National Secular Society that religious leaders are most likely to be "out of touch with" popular opinion "in matters of sexual ethics". The evidence surveyed so far in this section indicates a considerable degree of support for this claim. Williams' opinions on euthanasia and abortion appear to have been significantly out of line with popular opinion. Whilst it is true that public opinion was relatively divided in some other cases, such as Runcie's engagement on abortion-related issues and Carey's comments on the age of consent for gay men, even in these cases the Archbishop's stance clearly jarred against the direction of public opinion, which was becoming more liberal.

> "His contribution was yet another intellectual contortion to mollify his church's, Daily Mail wing instead of standing up for whatever it is he thinks."

Yet the public opinion data also highlight some surprising features of the Archbishop's engagement with these issues. In a number of cases, public opinion should have allowed the Archbishop to take a more conservative stance than he did. It is curious, for instance, that Carey chose to defend single mothers after the "back to basics" campaign. According to the British Social Attitudes survey, public opinion towards single mothers was rather mixed in 1994, the year after the Conservative conference in which the campaign was announced. On the question of whether "unmarried mothers get too little sympathy from society", opinion was fairly evenly split between those who disagreed (32 percent) and those who agreed (29 percent). When presented with the statement that "unmarried mothers who find it hard to cope have only themselves to blame", opinion was more sympathetic, with 47 percent disagreeing and 28 percent agreeing. In any case, these data hardly indicate a groundswell of popular sympathy. Runcie's approach to Section 28 in 1988 is even more perplexing. Although the survey does not record attitudes to same-sex relations in that year, data for the previous year was the most conservative on record, with 64 percent stating that same-sex relations are always wrong and just 11 percent judging them to be never wrong.

It is also revealing to observe how the press reported archiepiscopal activity on this issue. As might be expected, the Archbishop attracted criticism from some in the liberal press. Writing in The Guardian about the repeal of Section 28, for instance, Peter Preston responded critically to Carey's statement that society should "resist placing homosexual relationships on an equal footing with marriage".[225] Commenting on Williams' 2007 Observer article about abortion, Polly Toynbee penned a scathing critique in The Guardian: "His contribution was yet another intellectual contortion to mollify his church's woman-hating, gay-bashing, Daily Mail wing instead of standing up for whatever it is he thinks."[226] Whatever else may be said of the Archbishop's contribution to this area, it cannot be seen as an attempt to win over liberal sympathies.

Yet neither did the Archbishop win many friends from the right. Following comments by Carey on the topic, the Daily Mail responded by claiming that he was in line with public opinion. "The Archbishop of Canterbury is to be congratulated for firmly condemning adultery. Most people in this supposedly secular and permissive age still do."[227] Despite such positive write-ups, however, even he was criticised for being too liberal or too inactive on such issues. According to a report in *The Guardian*, Conservative minister John Redwood criticised the Church for neglecting marriage and focusing instead on other political issues such as urban poverty.[228] In response to Carey's defence of single mothers in 1993, Andrew Alexander responded in the *Daily Mail*, "[b]lame is, or should be, the Church's business. What is sin without blame?"[229] Three years later, the same paper commended the Archbishop for "his campaign to reverse Britain's moral decline", but also criticised him for his support of no-fault divorce and for failing to criticise "the infidelities admitted by both Prince Charles and Princess Diana".[230]

Despite being out of line with popular opinion, there is also surprising evidence that public opinion supported the Archbishop's right to speak out on these policy areas. The *European Values Study* records British opinion in 1990 about the legitimacy of the churches speaking out on several traditional moral issues. A slim majority of those expressing a view thought it appropriate for the churches to comment on extramarital affairs (49 percent agreed, 45 percent disagreed), while the same proportion thought it inappropriate for them to comment on homosexuality (49 percent disagreed, 43 percent agreed). On abortion, net agreement was greater, with 53 percent in agreement and 41 percent disagreeing. Support was greatest on euthanasia, with 57 percent agreeing and just 35 percent disagreeing.

Much of the Archbishop's participation in political debate about traditional moral issues was out of line with popular opinion, and his interventions certainly contradicted the direction of popular opinion. Nevertheless, his political activism in this area was not exclusively conservative, to the extent that he was sometimes criticised by some of the more morally conservative sections of the media. There is also very little evidence that he used this topic of debate to further the Church's interests, such as by enhancing the Church's popularity. Taken as a whole, however, it seems fair to conclude that this is a policy area in which archiepiscopal interventions are most vulnerable to the accusations of being outdated and unrepresentative of popular opinion. How serious an accusation this is, is a question that will be returned to in the final chapter of this report.

children and education

Throughout this period, the Archbishop participated in public policy debate about children and education. Although this section considers his input into this area of debate as a whole, it focuses on those aspects of education policy that are connected most closely to the Church's institutional interests, namely faith schools and religious education. Aside from its regular religious services, education is one of the Church's most significant spheres of activity. Figures from 2010 suggest that the Church's network of schools accounts for around one quarter of all maintained primary schools and six percent of all state-funded secondary schools in England.[231] Across England's schools more broadly, the

Church has vested interests in the teaching of religious education, which is part of the basic curriculum in England, and in the requirement that schools perform a daily act of collective worship.[232] More than in any area so far considered in this report, the Church has clear interests at stake in public policy relating to children and education.

All three officeholders were strongly supportive of the Church's role in education. Towards the start of this period, in 1982, Runcie emphasised his support for Church schools in a speech to the National Society for Promoting Christian Education, an organisation that represents Church schools.[233] Carey continued Runcie's lead, and in a speech to head teachers of Church primary schools in 1998 he celebrated their "tremendous contribution to Church and nation".[234] Towards the end of Carey's archiepiscopate, the Church commissioned a review of its network of schools, with Williams, who was at the time Archbishop of Wales, one of the members of the review team. The resulting report, *The Way Ahead*, recommended that Church schools pay greater attention to how they can be distinctively Christian, and that the Church significantly expand its involvement in the secondary sector.[235] As might be expected, Williams continued to follow this approach as Archbishop of Canterbury. Early in his tenure, for instance, he defended religious schools, including Muslim ones.[236] In a speech to the National Anglican Schools Conference, in 2006, he offered a robust defence of the work of Church schools against common objections.[237]

The Archbishop also engaged in debate about the treatment of religion in England's schools more broadly. When the Education Reform Bill reached committee stage in the Lords in 1988, Runcie delivered a speech about its provisions relating to religious education.[238] He also cast five votes on the legislation - one third of his total as Archbishop - although the extent to which they directly related to the Church's institutional interests is not immediately clear.[239] During the passage of the Further Education and Reform Bill through the Lords in 1992, Carey participated in a debate in which he warned against the "further loosening of the underpinnings of religious education".[240] He cast two votes on the legislation, one of which sought to ensure that collective worship would continue to be required in sixth form colleges.[241] Four years later, Carey opened a Lords debate on the topic of *Society's Moral and Spiritual Well-Being*, during which he voiced concerns that only twenty percent of secondary schools held a daily act of worship.[242] Although Williams did not engage with these issues in the Lords during this period, he did raise them in other contexts. For instance, in 2004 he delivered a speech at Downing Street in which he made suggestions for how religious education classes could better teach children about the realities of religious faith, including questions of doubt.[243]

The available public opinion data on religious schools reveal some contradictory findings. An ICM poll about race issues in 2001 found that 57 percent of the population supported the Church of England having state-funded schools in Britain, but found lower support for schools run by other religious groups.[244] In 2006, the *British Social Attitudes* survey reported 45 percent support for "churches or faith organisations" "getting more involved with schools", easily outweighing the 29 percent who opposed it. When asked by Populus in 2006 whether "[r]eligion and religious teaching should be kept out of schools that are funded by taxpayers money", 61 percent disagreed and just 36 percent agreed. Again, on the suggestion that "Catholic and Church of England schools are not a problem, but Muslim schools are more worrying because they help to keep Muslim communities apart from the rest of society", slightly more people agreed (47 percent) than disagreed (44 percent).[245] When asked whether the education of all children should include "a daily religious assembly and prayers", opinion was almost evenly split, with 45 percent in agreement and 44 percent in disagreement.[246]

Some other polling data, however, appear to partially contradict this apparent support. Despite apparently supporting Church schools, respondents to the Populus poll nevertheless agreed that faith schools are divisive (62 percent to 33 percent).[247] An ICM poll prior to the 2005 general election reported that 64 percent believed that "[s]chools should be for everyone regardless of religion and the government should not be funding faith schools of any kind", compared to 33 percent who agreed that "[f]aith schools are an important part of our education system."[248] When the same question was asked in 2010, opposition had fallen marginally to 59 percent, while support had increased slightly to 37 percent.[249] It is possible that by including in the option the statement that "[s]chools should be for everyone regardless of religion" the poll may have inflated the degree of opposition, although the finding is nevertheless significant. Indeed, a 2009 poll by YouGov reported strong opposition to selecting pupils on the basis of religious faith.[250] Towards the very end of this period, Ipsos MORI found in 2010 that only 4 percent thought "the most appropriate group to run state-funded schools" was religious organisations, while 35 percent – more than for any other option – responded that religious groups should not be permitted to run state schools.[251] Once again, however, this still leaves open the possibility that more than half the sample thought it legitimate for religious organisations to run schools. On the whole, it seems probable that the population was broadly accepting of the Church's role in education, although not uncritically so, with greater resistance gathering around the broader issue of 'faith' and 'religious' schools and perhaps particular resistance towards Muslim schools. The evidence for the Archbishop's input being outdated or unrepresentative is thus far from compelling.

> The Archbishop's defence of Church schools has often been criticised on the grounds that it is motivated by self-interest.

Predictably, Church and faith schools have been the subject of significant disagreement among press commentators. Writing for the *Daily Mail*, Stephen Glover praised their contribution. "By every imaginable yardstick these schools are more successful than those with no religious character – which explains why so many nonreligious parents want their children to go to them."[252] By contrast, *The Guardian*'s Zoe Williams called for their public funding to be revoked. "For a start, they are cherrypicking middle-class children [...] and, much more important, in many cases they are prosecuting an agenda that is repugnant. Are we really happy to sit back and pay for this?"[253]

As might be expected, the Church's role in education – and the Archbishop's defence of Church schools – has often been criticised on the grounds that it is motivated by self-interest. At the end of 2003, and shortly after Williams called for the government to allow the creation of new faith schools, the National Secular Society published a New Year's message to the Archbishop. Among many other criticisms, it described his "incursion into our education system" as "a cynical exercise in self-perpetuation".[254] Following his speech to the National Anglican Schools Conference in 2006, the NSS again objected. "The most vociferous proponents of keeping or expanding faith schools are those with a vested interest. It is no surprise that the Archbishop is so keen on these schools. His Church has got most to gain from them."[255]

It is quite clear that the Church does have vested institutional interests in education policy. As the sociologist Grace Davie has observed, religious education is an important "carrier" of religious tradition within a society.[256] Even so, the three officeholders denied that the Church's interests formed the primary motivation behind this strand of their political activity. Runcie argued that a goal of Church schools is to help children to understand the Christian approach to life rather than to secure their allegiance.[257] In his speech to National Anglican School Conference, Williams rejected the charge of "indoctrination". Like Runcie, he argued that religious schools allow children to develop understanding of religion from experience and participation – "schools for which religion is not a matter of external observation only" – so that "when a child who has been educated in such an environment makes adult decisions about religious commitment, there is at least a fair chance that they will know what it is they are deciding about."[258] When discussing the history of Church schools, Carey stated that they weren't primarily intended "to create and nurture good Anglicans", though he added "I believe that is an aim which should not be ignored." The primary purpose, he contended, was to help children develop "a life which was more satisfying – morally, spiritually and physically."[259] The officeholders also defended the Church's schools as expressions of service to the poor and disadvantaged. Runcie commented that they "often stand alongside the poor and deprived",[260] while Williams pointed out in a media interview that, contrary to popular opinion, the majority of the Church's newly-established schools "are in areas of deprivation, with very clear commitments and admissions policy [...] to the local community."[261]

Whatever the vested interests may have been, it is clear that the Archbishop did not seek to use Church schools in order to compete against other religious groups. The poll data outlined above suggest that the English population is more supportive of Church schools than those of minority religions, and so it would have been easy for officeholders to campaign strongly for Church as opposed to 'faith' schools. It is therefore interesting to note that Williams chose to also support the establishment of schools run by minority religious groups, which were less popular among the public. A similar story could be told about religious education and the passage of the Education Reform Bill in 1987-88. The Archbishop initially resisted any reference in the bill to the primacy of the Christian faith, which he warned could cause "unintended damage" to other religious groups.[262] Kenneth Baker, who was then the Education Secretary, reports that the Bishop of London (who led the Church's activity on this issue) agreed to strengthen the reference to Christianity only under pressure from other peers.[263] This casts some doubt on the charge that the Church's education policy was seen primarily in terms of institutional interests.

So, although it is difficult to deny that the Church had institutional interests at stake, and that these interests must have influenced the Archbishop to an extent, there are also indications that they do not tell the whole story. Rather than considering the Archbishop's support for religious education in isolation, it is helpful to see it as simply one component of his broader attitude to child and education policy. This wider context helps to illuminate some more recognisably moral motivations.

Both Runcie and Carey argued that particular attention should be paid to the teaching of moral values in all subjects.[264] Interestingly, it seems likely that the population as a whole was *less* sympathetic to these aspects of education than was the Archbishop. When asked for the *British Social Attitudes* survey in 1996 whether "[s]chools should spend more time teaching children right from wrong, even if it means less time is spent on basic subjects like reading and arithmetic", a significantly greater proportion disagreed (49 percent) than agreed (26 percent).

More broadly, all three officeholders argued that education should support children in the development of the whole person rather than being focused on narrow academic achievement. Runcie told the Synod that "[t]he Church's voice needs to be heard in education, expressing concern for the development of the whole person."[265] Carey likewise observed that education should not be restricted to providing children with "the right skills and aptitudes to take on our economic competitors", but must also help them to understand "what it means to be a good citizen and a moral person".[266] In a speech in 2005, Williams argued that the education system must facilitate emotional, moral and spiritual development in addition to academic progression.[267] Williams also addressed the development of children more generally on a large number of occasions,[268] including by raising concerns that rigorous testing has made education "anxiety driven" for many children.[269]

It is possible to understand the Church's schools as being a way of putting this vision for education into practice, rather than being simply a bald attempt to secure a new generation of the faithful. Runcie perhaps put this suggestion most cogently when he suggested that "a church school needs to be an explicit protest against any view of education and achievement which puts the accent on success in financial and status terms."[270] Carey likewise commented that Church schools "must challenge some of the prevailing assumptions of our culture" such as the view that education is solely a "preparation for work",[271] while Williams said that Church educational institutions should "model something better and more creative for our educational future."[272]

Given that the Archbishop is one of the most senior representatives of religious schools, it is not reasonable to argue that his contribution was irrelevant to political debate on this issue. Neither, on the whole, does it seem plausible that the Archbishop's support for religious schools was particularly out of line with popular opinion, although public opinion may have given a lower priority to moral education than the Archbishop did. The most convincing objection is that the Archbishop used this area of debate to further the institutional interests of the Church, both by expanding its reach into the education system and, by extension, forming of a new generation of practising (or at least nominal) Anglicans. While it is hard to deny this altogether, there is also good evidence to show that that the Archbishop regarded these institutional interests as being a way of promoting and enacting a moral vision for education policy.

religious policy

The final policy area considered in this report is public policy relating to religion. Into this category falls a range of issues, including religious groups' receipt of public funds, Sunday trading regulations, religious exemptions from the law, blasphemy legislation, the regulation of minority religious groups, and the continued establishment of the Church. Given that the Archbishop is England's leading religious spokesman, it is clear that his input into this area of debate was neither unnecessary nor irrelevant. It is possible that his contributions were unrepresentative of public opinion, although there are insufficient data to assess whether this is so for the whole range of topics in this section. The most plausible criticism of the Archbishop's intervention in this area is that it was motivated by the Church's institutional interests (its membership base, financial resources and its social authority), both to promote its own interests and to limit the power of its religious competitors. It is this objection that is the focus of this section.

It is undeniable that the Archbishop's political activism was, in some instances, primarily motivated by the Church's institutional interests. As Appendix 1 shows, five of the Lords debates that the Archbishop contributed to during this period related to the operation of the Church, including his defence of its use of a prayer book in contemporary language and the ordination of divorced and female clergy. However, the only reason these issues are "political" in the first place is because, as the established religion, the Church is subject to the Sovereign through Parliament.

Another clear – and probably more contentious – example is the Archbishop's appeals for financial assistance from the state. When, in 1990, a survey of the Church's cathedrals indicated that it would need to spend £70m over the following decade on preservation work, Runcie wrote to Margaret Thatcher to request a financial contribution from the state.[273] The government responded by announcing the provision of £11.5 million over three years for churches, of which the Church of England was expected to be the main beneficiary.[274] A decade later, the government announced its intention to reduce the cost of VAT on church repairs, and the following year confirmed that it would instead offset these costs by an equivalent amount. A press release from Lambeth Palace confirmed that the move had been in response to requests by Carey and others.[275] It is clear that, in this case, the Church's financial resources were enhanced by the Archbishop's lobbying of political leaders.

Williams' support for religious exemptions from the Equality Bill in 2010 can also be understood as a relatively clear expression of self-interest. The legislation would have restricted the ability of religious organisations to discriminate on the basis of compliance to the religion's teachings (for example on sexual behaviour) when appointing to some positions of employment. Key elements of the bill were rejected by the Lords and in one case the government would not have been defeated had the bishops not voted. In a subsequent press release, the National Secular Society claimed that "[t]he bishops voted entirely in their own interests".[276] Although the Archbishop did not directly participate in the vote, he did voice similar concerns in a speech to the General Synod.[277]

As an aside, however, it is significant that the Church's self-interest does not so readily explain Williams' support for similar exemptions from the Sexual Orientation Regulations in 2007, which outlawed discrimination on the basis of sexuality in the provision of goods or services. The Catholic Church protested that its adoption agencies should be exempt on the grounds that placing children with gay parents contradicted its religious teachings; the Church of England, by contrast, was apparently unconcerned about the implications for its own adoption agencies.[278] Yet Williams and the Archbishop of York nevertheless wrote a joint letter to the Prime Minister, supporting the Catholic position that "[t]he rights of conscience cannot be made subject to legislation" and adding that their opposition was motivated by the "interests of vulnerable children".[279] When the bishops failed to vote down the Regulations *en masse* in the Lords, a National Secular Society spokesman made the curious and unlikely suggestion that this, too, was a reflection of the Church's interests, because "a show of brute power would seriously jeopardise the survival of the Bishops Bench in House of Lords reform."[280] What it in fact shows is that the Archbishop has often defended the religious sector as a whole rather than the Anglican patch specifically, a theme that runs throughout this area of policy.

In addition to these clear displays of institutional self-interest, there are a number of cases where it seems likely that the Church's interests formed a significant motivation behind the Archbishop's political intervention, but in combination with moral concerns. A good example is Sunday trading legislation. In 1985-86, the Archbishop joined other Christian leaders in opposing elements of the government's ill-fated Shops Bill, including in the Lords.[281] In this instance, the churches' activism seems not to have been welcomed by the right-leaning press. The *Daily Mail* commended the government for "listening to the voice of the people",[282] while *The Daily Telegraph* dismissed the "alliance of churchmen and trade unionists".[283]

In 1994, the government returned to the issue of Sunday trading with the Sunday Trading Bill. The Archbishop again expressed concerns about aspects of the legislation, including by speaking and voting twice in the Lords.[284] When participating in this area of debate, both officeholders emphasised the impact of the legislation on society, and in particular on the most vulnerable. Runcie spoke of the "unfortunate effects on the most vulnerable members of our society and on family life",[285] while Carey commented that "[a] free-for-all is not always the same thing as the common good."[286] Whilst this moral explanation may seem plausible, it is difficult to deny that it is closely bound up with the Church's institutional interests, and in particular with what Carey later acknowledged as the "inevitable impact on Sunday attendance".[287]

A similar assessment might be reasonably made of Carey's decision to lobby the government for the celebrations at the Millennium Dome to have a Christian element. He initially raised the matter in the House of Lords in 1997,[288] and there was even talk of the Archbishop and his Catholic counterpart hosting an alternative celebration at a London cathedral if the government did not accede.[289] Although this relates to the social status of Christianity rather than of the Church itself, it is nevertheless closely connected to the Church's institutional interests. It appears that on this issue the Archbishop was in line with public opinion. In April 1999, Carey issued a press release following the publication of an opinion poll, commissioned by the Church, which reported that 58 percent supported the inclusion of a "Christian moment of reflection" in the Dome celebrations, compared to 37 percent who said there should not be.[290]

A further topic on which the Archbishop's stance was plausibly motivated by both institutional interests and moral concerns is the Church's establishment as the official state religion. On the face of it, establishment secures for the Church a social status that is denied to other groups, as well as privileges such as 26 seats in the Lords. According to the National Secular Society, the Church thus has a "vested interest in maintaining the *status quo*".[291] It seems particularly likely that establishment may enhance the Church's nominal membership base: nominal Christians in England associate overwhelmingly with the Church of England, with Anglican churches performing around half of all infant baptisms in the UK and around two-thirds of religious marriages in England and Wales.[292] There is also some evidence that both Runcie and Williams became more publicly supportive of establishment once they had been installed as Archbishop, which could be interpreted as the Church's interests trumping private conviction.[293]

Yet it should also be recognised that the officeholders' primary justification for establishment was that it allowed the Church better to serve the nation. Runcie, for instance, claimed that establishment places the Church "at the service of the whole nation, serving those in the outer court as well as those in the sanctuary",[294] while Carey commented that "establishment helps to underwrite the commitment of a national church to serve the entire community."[295] Likewise, Williams suggested that the Church's established status constitutes recognition by the state that politics is "answerable to more than narrowly political interest", and that "everyone in the nation has a right to access some kind of spiritual service".[296] It should also be remembered that, as well as conferring some advantages on the Church, establishment also brings disadvantages, such as restrictions on its autonomy, as the NSS acknowledges.[297] In addition, as Grace Davie has observed – and this report supports her analysis – the Church's contingent in the Lords has often used its access to "brin[g] to public attention the everyday problems of the most disadvantaged groups in British society, groups which were underrepresented in the House of Commons".[298] Although institutional interests cannot reasonably be eliminated as an explanation, neither can the officeholders' moral concern for the common good.

> *There are some episodes of archiepiscopal political engagement on religious policy that appear to contradict the Church's institutional interests.*

There are also, however, some episodes of archiepiscopal political engagement on religious policy that appear to flatly contradict the Church's institutional interests. One example is the political debate around blasphemy legislation, which gave symbolic protection to the Christian faith but was rarely enforced. In an early submission to the Law Society, Runcie recommended its extension to non-Christian religions,[299] but later suggested that it be abolished and replaced with the offence of inciting religious hatred, which would apply to all religions.[300] In a lecture about religious hatred in 2008, Williams made the perhaps surprising claim that although "a powerful or dominant religious body" – presumably including the Church – has little need of protection, some minority faiths do need legal protection.[301] When the blasphemy legislation was finally repealed in 2008, the Archbishops of Canterbury and York wrote to the Communities Secretary making clear that they would not oppose the move, but asking for reassurance that sufficient "provisions are in place to afford the necessary protection to individuals and to society".[302] This appears to indicate a consistent concern for the rights of minority religions, apparently in direct opposition to the symbolic status of the Church.

The best – and most notorious – example of this was is Williams' lecture to the Royal Courts of Justice in 2008, in which he suggested the elements of sharia (Islamic) law should be incorporated into the British legal system. What is remarkable about this speech is that there does not appear to have been any direct way in which the Church's institutional interests were promoted. Senior politicians from each of the three main political parties lined up to denounce his proposals,[303] while an unscientific poll in the *Sun* reported that 96 percent of the public opposed his comments.[304] Williams achieved the dubious honour of being the subject of the *Sun's* front page headline on two consecutive days: *What a Burkha*, followed by *Bash the Bishop*.[305] Several press commentators criticised the fact that the Archbishop had chosen to defend Islam rather than his own Church. Amanda Platell wrote in the *Daily Mail*, "If one good thing is to come out of the Archbishop's absurdly naive comments, it should be to provoke a debate over the need to fight for our Christian nation before it's too late."[306] In the same newspaper, Melanie Phillips suggested that Williams should be replaced by the Bishop of Rochester, Michael Nazir-Ali, "who *is* trying to defend the religion and culture of this country".[307]

In the speech itself, Williams claimed that his argument was based on ideas that are "historically rooted in Christian theology", such as the Judeo-Christian belief in the equality of all humans before God. Presumably, the reason he agreed to deliver the lecture was that he believed he had a helpful contribution to make on a topic that, as he put it, "is very widely felt to be a growing challenge in our society".[308] However else one may view sharia-gate (as it came to be known) the Archbishop's intervention was quite clearly not motivated by the Church's vested institutional interests.

Taken as a whole, there is significant evidence that the Archbishop did engage in (some) issues of 'religious policy' during this period to promote or defend the interests of the Church. However, he does not appear to have done so at the expense of other religious groups and, in some cases, appears to have defended minority religious groups at the expense of his own Church's interests. There are at least two plausible explanations for this behaviour. The first is that, as a religious leader, the Archbishop recognises the importance of the spiritual dimensions of life and is prepared to promote them regardless of the particular religion in question. Runcie, for instance, commented that an "awareness of the transcendent" is "an essential constituent of being human".[309] The second is that, as an establishment figure with a particular responsibility for religion, the Archbishop may feel a sense of duty to work for religious harmony. In her study of religion in Western Europe, Grace Davie suggests that weak state religions that are no longer able to dominate society, such as the Church of England, often use their status to "represent" the "religious sector".[310] As was noted in the introduction, one of the Archbishop's responsibilities is for inter-faith dialogue, and both Carey and Williams have said that they were surprised at the extent of this component of the Archbishop's role.[311] Although undeniably bound up with the Church's interests, both of these characteristics could be understood in positive terms. Indeed, it is even plausible to suggest - particularly in the case of his support for smaller groups within the religious sector - that this is one of the Archbishop's most valuable contributions to political debate in England. It seems fair to conclude that the Archbishop's engagement with this area was very often motivated in part by the institutional interests of the religious sector, but that this does not necessarily undermine its value.

chapter 2 references

1. Archbishop of Canterbury's Commission on Urban Priority Areas, *Faith in the City: A Call for Action by Church and Nation* (London: Church House Publishing, 1985).

2. Ibid. p. 205.

3. See Raymond Plant, "Conservative Capitalism: Theological and Moral Challenges," in *Theology in the City: A Theological Response to Faith in the City*, ed. Anthony Harvey (London: SPCK, 1989).

4. Archbishop of Canterbury's Advisory Group on Urban Priority Areas, *Living Faith in the City: A Progress Report* (London: General Synod of the Church of England, 1990), p. 88.

5. Bishops' Advisory Group on Urban Priority Areas, *Staying in the City: Faith in the City Ten Years On* (London: Church House Publishing, 1995), p. 31.

6. Commission on Urban Life and Faith, *Faithful Cities: A Call for Celebration, Vision and Justice* (Peterborough: Methodist Publishing House & London: Church House Publishing, 2006).

7. Robert Runcie, speech to the House of Lords, 2 February 1987, in *Parliamentary Debates*, Lords, vol 484, cc. 34-38.

8. George Carey, speech to the House of Lords, 22 May 1991, in *Parliamentary Debates*, Lords, vol 529, cc. 273-276.

9. Rowan Williams, speech to the House of Lords, 19 May 2006, in *Parliamentary Debates*, Lords, vol 682, cc. 501-506.

10. Anne Jacobs, George Jones and Des O'Sullivan, "Church Report 'Marxist': Anglican Commission Report on Inner Cities," 1 December 1985, *The Sunday Times*.

11. "Proposals Likely to Be Ignored," 2 December 1985, *The Times*.

12. "A Flawed Faith," 3 December 1985, *The Times*.

13. Digby Anderson, "Dogma Before Doing Good," 10 December 1985, *The Times*.

14. "The Shepherds Are Lost, Too," 2 December 1985, *Daily Mail*.

15. "You Can Throw Commonsense At the Problem," 3 December 1985, *The Guardian*.

16. Early Day Motion 192, 1985-6.

17. Robert Runcie, speech to the General Synod, 5 February 1986, *Report of Proceedings* 17:1 (London: Church House, 1986), p. 121.

18. "Faith and Works," 30 January 1990, *The Times*.

19. Clifford Longley, "Church Tempers its Criticism with Government Praise," 30 January 1990, *The Times*.

20. Walter Schwarz, "Church Renews Attack on Cities Policy," 30 January 1990, *The Guardian*.

21. Ruth Gledhill, "Church Finds 'Sea of Indifference' has Left Inner Cities," 17 November 1995, *The Times*.

22. Madeleine Bunting, "Critics Attack 'Bland' Church Poverty Report," 17 November 1995, *The Guardian*.

23. Ruth Gledhill, "Archbishop in Call for Action on Age of False Celebrity," 20 May 2006, *The Times*, http://www.timesonline.co.uk/tol/news/uk/article722169.ece; Maev Kennedy, "Government Accused of Draconian Treatment of Asylum Seekers," 23 May 2006, *The Guardian*, http://www.guardian.co.uk/news/2006/may/23/1.

24. Mark Gould, "Poor Understanding," interview of Fran Beckett, 7 June 2006, *The Guardian*, http://www.guardian.co.uk/society/2006/jun/07/socialexclusion.guardiansocietysupplement.

25. Edward Lucas, "A Capital Gain for Everyone," 25 May 2006, *The Times*.

26. The earnings disregard is the amount of money a person can earn before being losing their benefit.

27. Gould, "Poor Understanding," *The Guardian*.

28. Hugo Young, "No Government Answer to Faith in the City," 5 December 1985, *The Guardian*.

29. Cit. in *Faithful Cities*, p. 13.

30. George Carey, speech to FWA Colloquium, 21 February 1994, "Poverty and Exclusion," http://glcarey.co.uk/Speeches/1994/PovertyExclusion.html.

31. "Analysis and Review of the Church Urban Fund's 'Day in the Life' Project" (Coventry: SURGE, 2008), http://www.cuf.org.uk/sites/default/files/Day%20in%20Life%202007-08.pdf, p. 18.

32. Brierley, *Religious Trends 6*, p. 5.17.

33. Runcie, speech to General Synod, 5 February 1986, p. 122.

34. *Faith in the City*, p. 208.

35. Robert Runcie, speech to the House of Lords, 4 February 1982, in *Parliamentary Debates*, Lords, vol 426, cc. 1412, 1415.

36. Eric James, letter to editor, 27 May 1981, *The Times*.

37. Eric James, "Facing Both Ways: Runcie's Social Vision," in *Runcie: On Reflection*, ed. Stephen Platten (Norwich: Canterbury Press, 2002), p. 45.

38. Carey, speech to the Lords, 22 May 1991, c. 273.

39. Grace Davie, *Religion in Britain Since 1945: Believing Without Belonging* (Oxford: Blackwell, 1994), p. 152.

40. "A Flawed Faith," *The Times*.

41. Cit. in "You Can Throw," *The Guardian*.

42. Young, "No Government Answer, " *The Guardian*.

43. See Kenneth Leech, "The Church and Immigration and Race Relations Policy," in *Church and Politics Today: Essays on the Role of the Church of England in Contemporary Politics*, ed. George Moyser (Edinburgh: T&T Clark, 1985).

44. Robert Runcie, speech to the House of Lords, 22 June 1981, in *Parliamentary Debates*, Lords, vol 421, c. 875.

45. Ibid. c. 876.

46. Robert Runcie, speech to the House of Lords, 20 October 1981, in *Parliamentary Debates*, vol 421, c. 718.

47. Runcie, speech to the Lords, 22 June 1981, cc. 877, 878.

48. See Appendix 1.

49. Amendment 2 to Clause 1, on 7 July 1981.

50. George Carey and Basil Hume, letter to editor, 13 November 1991, *The Times*.

51. See Appendix 1.

52. George Carey, Basil Hume and KM Richardson, letter to editor, 15 July 1996, *The Times*.

53. "Archbishop Calls for Tolerance in Face of Kosovo Refugee Crisis," news release, 21 April 1999, http://web.archive.org/web/20021204030244/http://www.archbishopofcanterbury.org/releases/990421.htm.

54. Rowan Williams, speech to General Synod, 13 February 2004, "General Synod: Debate on Asylum – Archbishop of Canterbury's Remarks," http://www.archbishopofcanterbury.org/1193.

55. Rowan Williams, speech to the House of Lords, 15 February 2006, in *Parliamentary Debates*, Lords, vol 678, c. 1151.

56. "Williams: 'Immoral' to Send Asylum-Seekers Home," 28 June 2005, *The Daily Telegraph*, http://www.telegraph.co.uk/news/1492954/Williams-immoral-to-send-asylum-seekers-home.html.

57. "Attitudes Towards Immigration," Ipsos MORI, April 2008, http://www.ipsos-mori.com/researchpublications/researcharchive/poll.aspx?oItemId=53&view=wide.

58. "Asylum Poll," Ipsos MORI, January 2001, http://www.ipsos-mori.com/researchpublications/researcharchive/poll.aspx?oItemId=1322.

59. "Change Nationality Bill, Says Runcie," 23 June 1981, *Daily Mail*; "Bishops' Bid to Change the Nationality Bill Defeated," 8 July 1981, *The Guardian*; "Archbishop Maintains Criticism of British Nationality Bill," 21 October 1981, *The Times*; "Nationality Bill Over Last Hurdle," 21 October 1981, *The Guardian*; John Carvel, "Archbishops Warn of Asylum Bill Injustice," 13 November 1991, *The Guardian*; "Archbishops Worried," 13 November 1991, *The Daily Telegraph*; John Carvel, "Baker Denies Plans to Play Race Card," 15 February 1992, *The Guardian*; Alan Travis, "Carey Pleas for Welfare to Asylum Seekers," 15 July 1996, *The Guardian*; "Bishops Urge Asylum Leeway," 15 July 1996, *Daily Mail*; Rachel Sylvester and George Jones, "MPs Vote to Keep Tough Benefit Rules for Refugees," 16 July 1996, *The Daily Telegraph*; Alexandra Frean, "Embrace the Refugees, says Archbishop," 1 January 1999, *The Times*; "Williams: 'Immoral' to Send," *The Daily Telegraph*.

60. "A Precious Right", 14 November 1991, *The Times*.

61. Christopher Morgan, "Beware, Christian Soldier on Warpath", 2 February 2003, *The Times*.

62. Patrick O'Flynn, "Archbishop Right to Voice Asylum Fears," 3 February 2003, *The Daily Express*.

63. Stephen Bates, "Archbishop Wades into Asylum Controversy," 3 February 2003, *The Guardian*, http://www.guardian.co.uk/uk/2003/feb/03/immigration.immigrationandpublicservices.

64. "Archbishop at Centre of Asylum Row," 2 February 2003, *Daily Mail*, http://www.dailymail.co.uk/news/article-158046/Archbishop-centre-asylum-row.html.

65. O'Flynn, "Archbishop Right," *The Daily Express*.

66. James Slack, "Carey Calls on Brown to Restrict Migration," 25 June 2007, *Daily Mail*, http://www.dailymail.co.uk/news/article-464145/Carey-calls-Brown-restrict-migration.html; "Unlimited Migration May Lead to Violence on Britain's Streets, Warns Former Archbishop of Canterbury," 11 September 2008, *Daily Mail*, http://www.dailymail.co.uk/news/article-1054703/Unlimited-immigration-lead-violence-Britains-streets-warns-Archbishop-Canterbury.html; Jonathan Petre, "Britishness is Under Threat from Brown, Warns Lord Carey," 2 November 2008, *Daily Mail*, http://www.dailymail.co.uk/news/article-1082423/Britishness-threat-Brown-warns-Lord-Carey.html; James Slack, "'I Fear for my Grandchildren' says Former Archbishop of Canterbury, as he Calls for Christian Values to be Defended," 7 January 2010, *Daily Mail*, http://www.dailymail.co.uk/news/article-1240875/70-million-Immigrant-fuelled-population-boom-damage-society-say-leading-public-figures.html.

67. Max Hastings, "It is not Extremist, or Fascist, or Illiberal to Demand Stringent Immigration Controls," 25 June 2007, *Daily Mail*, http://www.dailymail.co.uk/debate/columnists/article-464355/It-extremist-fascist-illiberal-demand-stringent-immigration-controls.html.

68. Jonathan Wynne-Jones, "Study Reveals Impact of Immigration on UK Faiths," 13 December 2009, *The Daily Telegraph*, http://www.telegraph.co.uk/news/newstopics/religion/6799755/Study-reveals-impact-of-immigration-on-UK-faiths.html.

69. Peter Brierley, *Pulling Out of the Nose Dive: A Contemporary Picture of Churchgoing: What the 2005 English Church Census Reveals* (London: Christian Research, 2006), p. 94.

70. Joe Phillips and Gerard Lemos, letters to editor, 4 February 2003, *The Guardian*, http://www.guardian.co.uk/theguardian/2003/feb/04/guardianletters2.

71. Runcie, speech to the Lords, 22 June 1981, c. 878.

72. Mark Souster, Ian Smith and Vijitha Yapa, "Mendis Loses Last Appeal for Asylum," 20 January 1989, *The Times*; Gareth Parry and Michael Morris, "Mendis Asylum Offer Thwarted," 21 January 1989, *The Guardian*; Martin Wroe, "Sunday's Only Hope Rests in his Room with a Pew," 26 February 1995, *The Observer*; Dipesh Gadher and Graham Hind, "Archbishop Gives Holy Reference to Asylum Teenager," 24 August 2003, *The Sunday Times*, http://www.timesonline.co.uk/tol/news/uk/article883087.ece.

73. "Archbishop Calls for Tolerance," news release, 21 April 1999; "Archbishop Reflects on Visit to Oakington Immigration Centre," news release, 20 February 2008, http://www.archbishopofcanterbury.org/1731.

74. Runcie, speech to the Lords, 22 June 1981, c. 877.

75. "Archbishop Supports Calls for End to Detention of Children Seeking Asylum," news release, 9 July 2008, http://www.archbishopofcanterbury.org/1883.

76. George Carey and Basil Hume, letter to editor, 13 November 1991, *The Times*.

77. Robert Runcie, lecture to the Prison Reform Trust, 21 November 1989, in *Reform Renewal and Rehabilitation: Some Personal Reflections on Prison by Dr Robert Runcie, Archbishop of Canterbury* (London: Prison Reform Trust, 1990); George Carey, lecture to the Prison Reform Trust, 9 May 1996, in *Restoring Relationships: The Purpose of Prisons* (London: Prison Reform Trust, 1996); Rowan Williams, lecture to the Prison Reform Trust, 1 February 2007, "Criminal Justice – Building Responsibility," http://www.archbishopofcanterbury.org/401.

78. Robert Runcie, speech to the House of Lords, 15 November 1983, in *Parliamentary Debates*, Lords, vol 444, cc. 1154-1159.

79. Rowan Williams, speech to the House of Lords, 26 March 2004, in *Parliamentary Debates*, Lords, vol 659, cc. 949.

80. Rowan Williams, speech to the House of Lords, 6 February 2008, in *Parliamentary Debates*, Lords, vol 698, c. 1048.

81. Robert Runcie, speech to the General Synod, 12 July 1983, in *Report of Proceedings* 14:2 (London: Church House, 1983), pp. 496-498.

82. Robert Runcie, "Foreword," in Adrian Speller *Breaking Out: A Christian Critique of Criminal Justice* (London: Hodder and Stoughton, 1986).

83. Robert Runcie, speech to the National Association of Victim Support Schemes, Manchester, 3 July 1987, transcript accessed at Lambeth Palace Library, p. 11.

84. Ruth Gledhill, "Carey Challenges Belief That Prison is Effective," 8 April 1995, *The Times*; Anthony Bevins, "33 Tory MPs Set to Trigger Early Challenge to Major," 9 April 1995, *The Observer*; Anthony Doran, "Too Many People Are Locked Up in our Prisons, says Carey," 8 April 1995, *Daily Mail*.

85. Rowan Williams, speech to the General Synod, 11 July 2004, "Intervention in the Debate on Rethinking Sentencing," http://www.archbishopofcanterbury.org/1061.

86. Rowan Williams, speech at Worcester Cathedral, 17 July 2006, "Speech on Penal Policy," http://www.archbishopofcanterbury.org/710.

87. Runcie, speech to NAVSS, 3 July 1987, p. 14.

88. Carey, lecture to PRT, 9 May 1996 , p. 5.

89. Runcie, speech to the Lords, 15 November 1983, cc1156; Runcie, speech to NAVSS, 3 July 1987, pp15-19; Carey, lecture to PRT, 9 May 1996, p. 13.

90. Runcie, lecture to PRT, 21 November 1989, p. 2.

91. Ibid, p. 4.

92. Ibid, p. 12.

93. Runcie, speech to General Synod, 12 July 1983, p. 497.

94. Carey, lecture to PRT, 9 May 1996, p. 7.

95. Runcie, lecture to PRT, 21 November 1989, p. 6.

96. Runcie, speech to the Lords, 15 November 1983, c. 1155.

97. Carey, lecture to PRT, 9 May 1996, p. 13.

98. Williams, speech to Lords, 26 March 2004, c. 948.

99. "Attitudes Towards Capital Punishment," Ipsos MORI, 6 August 1995, http://www.ipsos-mori.com/researchpublications/researcharchive/poll.aspx?oItemId=2243; Poll for Channel 4 death penalty drama, Ipsos MORI, July 2009, http://www.ipsos-mori.com/Assets/Docs/Polls/mediact-channel-4-death-penalty-drama-computer-tables.pdf.

100. "Attitudes to Crime & Prisons 2004," Ipsos MORI, 12 November 2004, http://www.ipsos-mori.com/researchpublications/researcharchive/poll.aspx?oItemId=633.

101. John Carvel, "Runcie Shame Over Jails," 22 November 1989, *The Guardian*; Clifford Longley, "Runcie Calls for Rethink on Jails," 10 April 1990, *The Times*; Paul Eastham, "Carey and Howard on Collision Course over the Power of Prison," 9 May 1996, *Daily Mail*; Ruth Gledhill and Jill Sherman, "Carey Attacks Howard over 'Wild Frontier' Policy of Revenge," 10 May 1996, *The Times*; Michael Smith, "Carey Attacks Prison 'Revenge': Society's Aim Should Be to Rise Above Punishment for its Own Sake, Says Archbishop," 10 May 1996, *The Daily Telegraph*; Alan Travis, "Carey Attacks 'Prison Works' Policies," 10 May 1996, *The Guardian*; Richard Ford, "Archbishop Criticises Labour for 'Obsession' with Jailing Offenders," 2 February 2007, *The Times*; Alan Travis, "Archbishop Blames Costly Penal Culture for Jails Crisis," 2 February 2007 *The Guardian*, http://www.guardian.co.uk/uk/2007/feb/02/ukcrime.prisonsandprobation; "More Pressure on Reid as Archbishop Attacks 'Worse Than Useless' Prisons," 1 February 2007, *Daily Mail* website, http://www.dailymail.co.uk/news/article-433105/More-pressure-Reid-Archbishop-attacks-worse-useless-jails.html.

102. Colin Brown, "In-House Briefing," 11 November 1983, *The Guardian*.

103. Clifford Longley, "Runcie Says Criminals Are Being Recycled," 4 July 1987, *The Times*; Tom Sharratt, "Runcie Blames Prison Terms for Hardened Criminals," 4 July 1987, *The Guardian*.

104. Malcolm Dean, "Too Many Criminal Offences, says Report," 7 April 1986, *The Guardian*.

105. See n84 above.

106. Michael Howard, "Our First Duty Must Always Be to the Victims," 10 April 1995, *Daily Mail*.

107. "Prison Horrors," 8 April 1995, *Daily Mail*.

108. "Crime and Dr Carey," 10 May 1996, *Daily Mail*.

109. Sean McConville et. al., letter to editor, 3 June 1996, *The Times*.

110. Runcie, lecture to PRT, 21 November 1989, p. 10.

111. Carey, lecture to PRT, 9 May 1996, p. 1.

112. Williams, speech to General Synod, 11 July 2004.

113. Philip Towle, *Going to War: British Debates from Wilberforce to Blair* (Basingstoke: Palgrave Macmillan, 2010), pp. 24-39.

114. Robert Runcie, speech to the House of Lords, 14 April 1982, in *Parliamentary Debates*, Lords, vol 429, cc. 298-299; Robert Runcie, speech to the House of Lords, 20 May 1982, in *Parliamentary Debates*, Lords, vol 430, cc. 814-815

115. Robert Runcie, sermon at St Paul's Cathedral, 26 July 1982, "The Falkland Islands," in Runcie *Windows onto God*, p. 109.

116. John Nott, *Here Today, Gone Tomorrow: Recollections of an Errant Politician* (London: Politico's, 2002) p. 317.

117. Robert Runcie, speech to the House of Lords, 6 September 1990, in *Parliamentary Debates*, Lords, vol 521, cc. 1807-1810; Robert Runcie, speech to the House of Lords, 15 January 1991, in *Parliamentary Debates*, Lords, vol 524, cc. 1097-1100.

118. John Major, *John Major: The Autobiography* (London: HarperCollins, 1999), p. 232.

119. "I Do Not Link Islam and Terrorism," 9 November 2001, *The Church Times*

120. Carey, *Know the Truth*, pp. 211-213.

121. Carey interview with author.

122. Jamie Wilson, "Archbishop Warns on Iraq," 28 October 2002, *The Guardian*.

123. Shortt, *Rowan's Rule*, p. 259.

124. "Joint Statement on Iraq from the Archbishop and Cardinal", news release, 20 February 2003, http://www.archbishopofcanterbury.org/852.

125. Robert Runcie, "When the Price of Even a Just War Becomes Too High," 8 May 1982, *The Times*.

126. "Joint Statement by Religious Leaders on Conflict with Iraq," news release, 21 March 2003, http://www.archbishopofcanterbury.org/859.

127. Runcie, speech to the Lords, 15 January 1991, c. 1100.

128. Runcie, speech to the Lords, 14 April 1982, c. 299.

129. Runcie, speech to the Lords, 6 September 1990, c. 1809.

130. "Archbishop of Canterbury Interview with Al Jazeera TV, Qatar," news release, 5 November 2001, http://web.archive.org/web/20021204033559/http://www.archbishopofcanterbury.org/releases/011105.htm.

131. "Joint Statement," 21 March 2003.

132. Richard Harries, "The Continuing, Crucial Relevance of Just War Criteria," in *British Foreign Policy and the Anglican Church: Christian Engagement with the Contemporary World*, ed. Timothy Blewett, Adrian Hyde-Price and Wyn Rees (Aldershot: Ashgate, 2008).

133. Carpenter, *Reluctant Archbishop*, p. 249; Carey, interview with author; Towle, *Going to War*, p. 38.

134. Robert Runcie, lecture to the Royal Institute of International Affairs, Chatham House, 25 January 1983, "Just and Unjust Wars," in *Windows onto God*; Rowan Williams, lecture to the Royal Institute of International Affairs, Chatham House, 12 October 2003, "Just War Revisited", http://www.archbishopofcanterbury.org/1214.

135. Robert Runcie, "When the Price," *The Times*; "Archbishop of Canterbury's First Reaction to Hostilities," news release, 17 January 1991, accessed at Lambeth Palace Library.

136. Ruth Gledhill, "War Not Just, Carey Says," 14 February 1991, *The Times*.

137. "I Do Not Link," *The Church Times*.

138. Carey, interview with author.

139. "The Falklands War – Trends," Ipsos MORI, June 1982, http://www.ipsos-mori.com/researchpublications/researcharchive/poll.aspx?oItemId=47&view=wide.

140. Colin Rallings, Michael Thrasher & Nick Moon, "British Public Opinion During the Gulf War," in *Contemporary British History* 6:2 (1992), p. 380.

141. "Support for War in Afghanistan – Trends 2001," Ipsos MORI, 29 November 2001, http://www.ipsos-mori.com/researchpublications/researcharchive/poll.aspx?oItemId=2399&view=wide.

142. "War with Iraq – Trends (2006-2007)," Ipsos MORI, May 2007, http://www.ipsos-mori.com/researchpublications/researcharchive/poll.aspx?oItemId=55&view=wide.

143. Stephen Bates, Michael White and Anne Perkins, "Pressure Points," 15 January 2003, *The Guardian*, http://www.guardian.co.uk/politics/2003/jan/15/uk.conservatives.

144. "Blair and the Bishops," 21 February 2003, *The Guardian*, http://www.guardian.co.uk/world/2003/feb/21/religion.iraq.

145. "Out of Tune," *The Sun*.

146. "We Did Fight the Good Fight," 27 July 1982, *Daily Mail*.

147. Melanie Phillips, "This War Is About Good Versus Evil," 24 March 2003, *Daily Mail*, http://www.dailymail.co.uk/debate/columnists/article-229993/This-war-IS-good-versus-evil.html.

148. "Render unto Caesar," 27 December 2002, *The Daily Telegraph*, http://www.telegraph.co.uk/comment/telegraph-view/3585667/Render-unto-Caesar.html.

149. Donald Macintyre, "Is it Possible that Mr Blair will Not Back President Bush over Iraq?," 30 July 2002, *The Independent*, http://www.independent.co.uk/opinion/commentators/donald-macintyre/is-it-possible-that-mr-blair-will-not-back-president-bush-over-iraq-649886.html.

150. Stephen Bates, "Gallantry After the Battle," 25 January 2007, *The Guardian* website, http://www.guardian.co.uk/commentisfree/2007/jan/25/adoptanarchbishop.

151. Robert Runcie, speech to Global Forum of Spiritual and Parliamentary Leaders, 11 April 1988, "Human Survival," in *The Unity We Seek* (London: Darton, Longman and Todd, 1989), pp. 41-42; Robert Runcie, speech at the Lambeth Conference, 6 August 1988, "The Close of the Lambeth Conference," in *The Unity We Seek*, p. 28; Robert Runcie, sermon at Canterbury Cathedral, 25 December 1988, "Christmas," in *The Unity We Seek*, p. 155.

152. Robert Runcie, sermon at the Festival of Faith and the Environment, Canterbury Cathedral, 17 September 1989, transcript accessed at Lambeth Palace Library, p. 5.

153. George Carey, speech to the Green Party, Wells Town Hall, 20 March 1990, "God is Green," in *I Believe* (London: SPCK, 1991).

154. Sue Brattle, "An Eco-Plan of my Own," 6 June 1993, *The Guardian*.

155. George Carey, Millennium Lecture, Blackheath Concert Halls, 9 November 1999, "The Hinge of Time," http://web.archive.org/web/20021102113150/http://www.archbishopofcanterbury.org/speeches/991109.html.

156. "Archbishop of Canterbury's New Year Message," news release, 31 December 2000, http://web.archive.org/web/20021204032313/http://www.archbishopofcanterbury.org/releases/001231.htm.

157. "Joint Open Letter," news release, 25 May 2001.

158. "6 Days to Go", 29 April 2005, *The Guardian*, http://www.guardian.co.uk/politics/2005/apr/29/uk.election2005.

159. Rowan Williams, lecture at Lambeth Palace, 5 July 2004, "Changing the Myths We Live By," http://www.archbishopofcanterbury.org/1064.

160. Rowan Williams, speech at the General Synod, 17 February 2005, "Speech in Debate on the Environment," http://www.archbishopofcanterbury.org/1010.

161. Rowan Williams, speech to the World Council of Churches Assembly, Brazil, 18 February 2006, "Globalisation, Economics and Environment," http://www.archbishopofcanterbury.org/308.

162. "Archbishop Issues Letter," news release, 31 March 2005.

163. Rowan Williams and John Sentamu, "Archbishops' Article on the General Election," 29 April 2010, originally published in *The Church Times*, http://www.archbishopofcanterbury.org/2846.

164. "Church Leaders – A Climate Treaty for Climate Justice," news release, 30 November 2007, http://www.archbishopofcanterbury.org/1356.

165. "Climate Change Action a Moral Imperative for Justice," news release, 19 December 2007, http://www.archbishopofcanterbury.org/1366.

166. "Churches Urge Europe's Leaders to Build a Greener Economy," news release, 9 December 2008, http://www.archbishopofcanterbury.org/2060.

167. "Archbishop Urges Prayer for Planet on Environment Sunday – June 7," news release, 3 June 2009, http://www.archbishopofcanterbury.org/2437.

168. "Faith Leaders – Tackling Climate Change is a 'Moral Imperative'," news release, 29 October 2009, http://www.archbishopofcanterbury.org/2589.

169. Rowan Williams, sermon at Westminster Central Hall, 5 December 2009, "Environment Service at Westminster Central Hall, London," http://www.archbishopofcanterbury.org/2649.

170. Rowan Williams, sermon at Copenhagen Cathedral, 13 December 2009, "Act for the Sake of Love," http://www.archbishopofcanterbury.org/2675.

171. "Cardiff University, Energy Futures and Climate Change Survey 2010, Draft Topline," Ipsos MORI, 2010, http://www.ipsos-mori.com/Assets/Docs/Polls/climate-change-still-high-on-publics-agenda-topline.pdf, p. 4.

172. Ibid., p. 8.

173. Ibid., p. 12.

174. "Greening the Church," 18 September 1989, *The Times*.

175. Ruth Gledhill, "Primate Predicts Ecological Crisis," 6 July 2004, *The Times*; Paul Brown, "Climate Change Threatens Species, says Archbishop", 6 July 2004, *The Guardian*, http://www.guardian.co.uk/society/2004/jul/06/environment.religion; "Primate's Doomsday Warning," 6 July 2004, *The Daily Express*; Ruth Gledhill, "End of the World is Nigh, says Williams," 4 September 2009, *The Times*; Ruth Gledhill, "It's Your Responsibility Before God on Climate, says Williams," 29 March 2006, *The Times*; Ruth Gledhill, "The World is Not a Warehouse to Serve Our Greed, Archbishop Tells Worshippers," 26 December 2007, *The Times*; Riazat Butt, "Christian Leaders Call for Peace and Respect for Environment," 27 December 2007, *The Guardian*, http://www.guardian.co.uk/uk/2007/dec/27/religion.world; Riazat Butt, "Dr Rowan Williams says Climate Crisis a Chance to Become Human Again," 13 October 2009, *The Guardian*, http://www.guardian.co.uk/uk/2009/oct/13/rowan-williams-climate-crisis; Robin McKie and Bibi van der Zee, "Hundreds Arrested in Copenhagen as Green Protest March Leads to Violence," 13 December 2009, *The Observer*, http://www.guardian.co.uk/environment/2009/dec/13/hundreds-arrested-in-copenhagen-violence.

176. "Climate Change – Interview for the BBC Radio 4 *Today* Programme," transcript of broadcast on 28 March 2006, http://www.archbishopofcanterbury.org/357; "Environment – Ethical Man, BBC 2 Newsnight," transcript of broadcast on 4 May 2006, http://www.archbishopofcanterbury.org/376.

177. Zac Goldsmith, "Climate Change Brings us an Uncomplicated Choice," 31 August 2006, *The Guardian*, http://www.guardian.co.uk/commentisfree/2006/aug/31/comment.greenpolitics.

178. Richard Littlejohn, "Losing His Religion," 27 March 2009, *Daily Mail*.

179. Runcie, sermon at Festival of Faith, 17 September 1989, p. 7.

180. George Carey, speech at bishops' meeting, 4 June 2001, "Environmental Seminar," http://web.archive.org/web/20030122133416/http://www.archbishopofcanterbury.org/speeches/010604.htm.

181. Rowan Williams, "A New Spiritual Politics of Limits," 26 July 2008, *The Guardian* website, http://www.guardian.co.uk/commentisfree/2008/jul/26/climatechange.religion.

182. Rowan Williams, lecture for Operation Noah, Southwark Cathedral, 13 October 2009, "The Climate Crisis: Fashioning a Christian Response," http://www.archbishopofcanterbury.org/2565.

183. Robert Runcie, speech at seminar for the Commission for International Justice and Peace, Archbishop's House, 23 November 1982, "The Third World: A Christian Concern" in *Windows onto God*.

184. Jamie Wilson, "50,000 in Human Chain Reinforce Petition Shipped to G8 Leaders," 14 June 1999, *The Guardian*.

185. Stephen Bates, "Rich Impose Terms on Poor, says Williams," 27 April 2005, *The Guardian*, http://www.guardian.co.uk/society/2005/apr/27/internationalaidanddevelopment.debt.

186. Carey, speech at bishops' meeting, 4 June 2001.

187. Interview for Today Programme, 28 March 2006.

188. "Greening the Church," *The Times*.

189. Stephen Glover, "If Our Archbishop Spent Less Time Fretting about Climate Change, he Might Notice the Pope is About to Mug Him," 22 October 2009, *The Daily Mail*, http://www.dailymail.co.uk/debate/columnists/article-1222046/If-Archbishop-spent-time-fretting-climate-change-notice-pope-mug-him.html.

190. "Greening the Church," *The Times*.

191. Carey, Millennium Lecture, 9 November 1999.

192. Rowan Williams, "New Spiritual Politics," *The Guardian* website.

193. Warner, *Confessions*, pp. 81-82.

194. "Archbishop of Canterbury's Message to National Marriage Week," news release, 14 February 2000, http://web.archive.org/web/20021204032313/http://www.archbishopofcanterbury.org/releases/000214.htm; "Archbishop of Canterbury Supports National Marriage Week," news release, 25 January 2001, http://web.archive.org/web/20021204033559/http://www.archbishopofcanterbury.org/releases/0101252.htm; "Message from the Archbishop of Canterbury for National Marriage Week 2002," news release, 8 February 2002, http://web.archive.org/web/20021204032606/http://www.archbishopofcanterbury.org/releases/020208.htm.

195. George Carey, lecture at Liverpool John Moores University, 23 February 2000, "Christianity and Citizenship," http://web.archive.org/web/20030122132812/http://www.archbishopofcanterbury.org/speeches/000223.htm.

196. George Carey, "We Must Protect our Young Children," 22 July 1998, originally published in *The Times*, http://web.archive.org/web/20030122133647/http://www.archbishopofcanterbury.org/speeches/980722.htm.

197. See Appendix 1.

198. George Carey, sermon at Westminster Central Hall, 23 January 2000, "London Church Leaders – Capital Joy!," http://web.archive.org/web/20030122132812/http://www.archbishopofcanterbury.org/speeches/000123.htm.

199. Robert Runcie, speech to the General Synod, 12 July 1983, in *Report of Proceedings* 14:2 (London: Church House, 1983), pp. 447-449.

200. Robert Runcie, 2 July 1984, originally published in *The Times*, "Fighting Divorce with Faith," in *One Light for One World*.

201. *Parliamentary Debates*, Lords, vol 469, 9 December 1985, c. 43.

202. Rowan Williams, speech at the House of Commons, 5 February 2007, "Get a Life: Speech at Launch of National Marriage Week," http://www.archbishopofcanterbury.org/542.

203. "Archbishop – Good Childhood Report 'A Clarion Call' for Society," news release, 2 February 2009, http://www.archbishopofcanterbury.org/2154.

204. For example, see Rowan Williams, speech to the Gay and Lesbian Christian Movement, no date given, "The Body's Grace," http://www.igreens.org.uk/bodys_grace.htm.

205. Runcie, speech to General Synod, 12 July 1983, p. 447.

206. Robert Runcie, speech to the House of Lords, 3 July 1989, in *Parliamentary Debates*, Lords, vol 509, cc. 1012-1015.

207. Appendix 1, Local Government Bill.

208. Jasper Gerard, "Williams Casts Aside the Carey Hairshirt on Sex," 23 February 2003, *The Sunday Times*; "Sex Outside Marriage is No Sin, says Archbishop," 2 October 2002, *Daily Mail*, http://www.dailymail.co.uk/news/article-140843/Sex-outside-marriage-sin-says-Archbishop.html.

209. James Macintyre, "Interview: Rowan Williams," 18 December 2008, *New Statesman*, http://www.newstatesman.com/religion/2008/12/williams-archbishop-lambeth.

210. George Carey, speech to community leaders, Harrogate, 30 October 1992, "Christianity and a Vision for Society," in *Sharing a Vision*, Carey, p. 103.

211. Patrick Wintour and Walter Schwarz, "Cabinet Ire as Carey Backs Lone Mothers," 12 October 1993, *The Guardian*

212. George Carey, speech to Mother's Union, 3 November 1993, transcript accessed at Lambeth Palace Library, pp. 3, 5.

213. "Public Attitudes to Section 28," Ipsos MORI, February 2000, http://www.ipsos-mori.com/researchpublications/researcharchive/poll.aspx?oItemId=1576&view=print.

214. See Appendix 1, Instant Life (Preservation) Bill, and Human Fertilisation and Embryology Bill.

215. Bernard Levin, "Spectrum: Where is Our Moral Energy? – Interview with the Archbishop of Canterbury," 30 March 1987, *The Times*.

216. "Bishops Oppose 'Misguided and Unnecessary' Euthanasia Bill," Church of England, news release, 6 September 2004, http://www.churchofengland.org/media-centre/news/2004/09/news_item2004-10-199713099720.aspx.

217. Rowan Williams, "Does a Right to Assisted Death Entail a Responsibility on Others to Kill?," 20 January 2005, *The Times*, http://www.timesonline.co.uk/tol/comment/columnists/guest_contributors/article414581.ece.

218. Rowan Williams, speech to the House of Lords, 12 May 2006, in *Parliamentary Debates*, Lords, vol 681, cc. 1196-1198.

219. "Assisted Dying – The Today Programme," transcript of broadcast on 12 May 2006, http://www.archbishopofcanterbury.org/664; Rowan Williams, Cormac Murphy-O'Connor and Jonathan Sacks, letter to editor, 12 May 2006, *The Times*, http://www.timesonline.co.uk/tol/comment/letters/article716130.ece.

220. Rowan Williams, speech to the House of Lords, 15 January 2008, in *Parliamentary Debates*, Lords, vol 697, c. 1185-1186.

221. "Archbishop on Human Fertilisation and Embryology Bill," Press Association, 30 January 2008, http://www.archbishopofcanterbury.org/1639; Rowan Williams, "We Condemn Torture, Rape – Anything that Uses Another's Body for our own Purpose – Shouldn't we Show Embryos Similar Respect?," 11 May 2008, *Mail on Sunday*, http://www.dailymail.co.uk/news/article-565436/We-condemn-torture-rape--uses-anothers-body-purpose--Shouldnt-embryos-similar-respect.html.

222. Rowan Williams, "People are Starting to Realise we Can't go on as we Are," 20 March 2005, *The Sunday Times*, http://www.timesonline.co.uk/tol/news/article432254.ece.

223. Rowan Williams, "Britain's Abortion Debate Lacks a Moral Dimension," 21 October 2007, *The Observer*, http://www.guardian.co.uk/commentisfree/2007/oct/21/comment.religion.

224. "Attitudes to Abortion – Trends," Ipsos MORI, 28 November 2006, http://www.ipsos-mori.com/researchpublications/researcharchive/poll.aspx?oItemId=1147&view=wide.

225. Peter Preston, "My Daughter is Just Fine," 31 January 2000, *The Guardian*, http://www.guardian.co.uk/world/2000/jan/31/gayrights.comment.

226. Toynbee, "A Woman's Supreme Right," *The Guardian*.

227. "Home Truths," *Daily Mail*.

228. "Government Attacks Archbishop over 'Important Moral Issues'," 13 February 1993, *The Guardian*.

229. Andrew Alexander, "As Tough as Old Slippers?" 15 October 1993, *Daily Mail*.

230. "Morals, the Church and the Archbishop," 6 July 1996, *Daily Mail*.

231. "Schools, Pupils, and Their Characteristics, January 2010 (Provisional)," Department for Education, 13 May 2010, http://www.education.gov.uk/rsgateway/DB/SFR/s000925/sfr09-2010.pdf, p. 18.

232. For more information, see David McClean, "State and Church in the United Kingdom," in *State and Church in the Modern European Union*, second edition, ed. Gerhard Robbers (Baden-Baden: Nomos, 2005).

233. Robert Runcie, speech to the National Society, 17 March 1982, "Christian Education," in *Windows onto God*.

234. George Carey, speech at Church House, Westminster, 10 June 1998, "Archbishop of Canterbury's Address to Church of England Primary School Headteachers," http://web.archive.org/web/20030122133647/http://www.archbishopofcanterbury.org/speeches/980610.htm.

235. Church Schools Review Group, *The Way Ahead: Church of England Schools in the New Millennium* (London: Church House, 2001), http://www.churchofengland.org/media/1118777/way%20ahead%20-%20whole.pdf.

236. Rebecca Smithers, "Archbishop Defends Faith Schools," 12 September 2003, *The Guardian*, http://www.guardian.co.uk/education/2003/sep/12/schools.uk.

237. Rowan Williams, speech to the National Anglican Schools Conference, London, 14 March 2006, "Church Schools: A National Vision," http://www.archbishopofcanterbury.org/351.

238. Robert Runcie, speech to the House of Lords, 3 May 1988, in *Parliamentary Debates*, Lords, vol 496, cc. 510-512.

239. Appendix 1, Education Reform Bill.

240. George Carey, speech to the House of Lords, 3 February 1992, in *Parliamentary Debates*, Lords, vol 535, c. 62.

241. Appendix 1, Further and Higher Education Bill.

242. George Carey, speech to the House of Lords, 5 July 1996, in *Parliamentary Debates*, Lords, vol 573, cc. 1691-1695.

243. Rowan Williams, speech at Downing Street, 8 March 2004, "Belief, Unbelief and Religious Education," http://www.archbishopofcanterbury.org/1173.

244. "Race in Britain Poll November 2001," ICM Research, November 2001, http://www.icmresearch.co.uk/pdfs/2001_november_observer_race_poll.pdf.

245. "Faith Schools," Populus, 2006, http://populuslimited.com/uploads/download_pdf-261006-The-Daily-Politics-Faith-Schools.pdf.

246. "Faith Schools Survey for Channel 4," ICM Research, 2010, http://www.icmresearch.co.uk/pdfs/2010_august_c4_FaithSchools.pdf, p. 11.

247. "Faith Schools," Populus, 2006.

248. "Guardian Opinion Poll," ICM Research, August 2005, http://www.icmresearch.co.uk/pdfs/2005_august_guardian_august_poll.pdf, p. 20.

249. "Faith Schools Survey," ICM Research, 2010, p. 14.

250. "YouGov / Accord Coalition Survey Results," YouGov, June 2009, tranets/ygarchives/content/pdf/RESULTS%20for%20Accord%20Coalition%20%28School%20Worship%29.pdf.

251. "Who Should Run State Schools?," Ipsos MORI, 2010, http://www.ipsos-mori.com/Assets/Docs/Polls/poll-nasuwt-who-should-run-state-schools-topline.pdf.

252. Stephen Glover, "Why Are We Trying to Destroy Our Faith Schools?," 26 October 2006, *Daily Mail*, http://www.dailymail.co.uk/news/article-412709/Why-trying-destroy-faith-schools.html.

253. Zoe Williams, "Faith Schools Should Not be Tax-Funded and Here's Why," 19 September 2007, http://www.guardian.co.uk/commentisfree/2007/sep/19/comment.faithschools.

254. Terry Sanderson, "New Year's Message".

255. "Archbishop's Defence," National Secular Society.

256. Davie, *Religion in Britain*, p. 135.

257. Runcie, speech to National Society, 17 March 1982, pp. 81-83.

258. Williams, speech to NASC, 14 March 2006.

259. George Carey, speech to Anglican Secondary School Heads, Chester, 19 September 1991, "Education: Commitment, Co-operation and Challenge", in *Sharing A Vision*, p. 16.

260. Robert Runcie, speech to the General Synod, 3 July 1985, in *Report of Proceedings* 16:2 (London: Church House, 1985), p. 647.

261. Rusbridger, "Interview," *The Guardian* website.

262. Runcie, speech to the Lords, 3 May 1988, c. 512.

263. Kenneth Baker, *The Turbulent Years: My Life in Politics* (London: Faber and Faber, 1993), pp. 207-209.

264. Robert Runcie, speech to the National Confederation of Parent-Teacher Associations, Canterbury, 14 April 1984, "Morality in Education," in *One Light for One World*, p119; Carey, speech to Lords, 5 July 1996, cc. 1694-1695.

265. Runcie, speech to General Synod, 3 July 1985, p. 647.

266. Carey, speech to Lords, 5 July 1996, c. 1692.

267. Rowan Williams, lecture to Citizen Organising Foundation, London, 11 April 2005, "Formation: Who's Bringing Up our Children?," http://www.archbishopofcanterbury.org/911.

268. "Interview: The Good Childhood Inquiry," transcript of broadcast on BBC Radio 4, 18 September 2006, http://www.archbishopofcanterbury.org/626; "Commercialisation of Childhood," transcript of interview on BBC 1 Breakfast, 13 December 2006, http://www.archbishopofcanterbury.org/1313; Rowan Williams, speech to the House of Lords, 25 April 2008, in *Parliamentary Debates*, Lords, vol 700, cc1768-1772; "Good Childhood Report," news release, 2 February 2009; Rowan Williams, speech to the House of Lords, 12 February 2009, *Parliamentary Debates*, Lords, vol 707, cc. 1247-1250.

269. "Interview, "The Good Childhood Inquiry," 18 September 2006.

270. Runcie, speech to the National Society, 17 March 1982, p. 84.

271. Carey, speech to Anglican Secondary School Heads, 19 September 1991, pp. 24-25.

272. Rowan Williams, speech to the Church of England Academy Family Launch Conference, Lambeth Palace, 21 October 2009, "Christian Distinctiveness in our Academies," http://www.archbishopofcanterbury.org/2573.

273. "Runcie Calls for Cathedral Aid," 7 August 1990, *The Guardian*.

274. Martin Bailey, "State Aid for Britain's Crumbling Cathedrals," 11 November 1990, *The Observer*.

275. "Archbishop of Canterbury Welcomes Chancellor's Initiative to Reduce VAT on Church Repairs," news release, 8 November 2000, http://web.archive.org/web/20021204032313/http://www.archbishopofcanterbury.org/releases/001108.htm.

276. "Equality Bill Reforms Hit the Buffers as Bishops Derail Amendments," National Secular Society, news release, 29 January 2010, http://www.secularism.org.uk/equality-bill-reforms-hit-the-bu.html.

277. Rowan Williams, speech to the General Synod, 9 February 2010, "The Archbishop's Presidential Address", http://www.archbishopofcanterbury.org/2763.

278. Jonathan Petre and George Jones, "Churches Unite Against Gay Laws," 24 January 2007, http://www.telegraph.co.uk/news/uknews/1540369/Churches-unite-against-gay-laws.html.

279. "Equality Act Regulations: Letter from the Archbishops of Canterbury and York to the Prime Minister," news release, 23 January 2007, http://www.archbishopofcanterbury.org/416.

280. Terry Sanderson, "A Significant Event: Is the Tide Turning Against the Bishops?," National Secular Society, 23 March 2007, http://www.secularism.org.uk/78258.html.

281. John Carvel, "Whips Take Gamble over Sunday Shopping," 10 April 1986, *The Guardian*; Adam Raphael and Robert Taylor, "Counter Measures Split Sunday Lobby," 13 April 1986, *The Observer*; Robert Runcie, speech to the General Synod, 3 July 1985, in *Report of Proceedings* 16:2 (London: Church House, 1985), pp. 554-555; Robert Runcie, speech to the General Synod, 5 February 1986, in *Report of Proceedings* 17:1 (London: Church House, 1986), pp. 215-216; Robert Runcie, speech to the House of Lords, 18 April 1986, in *Parliamentary Debates*, Lords, vol 473, c. 877; for vote see Appendix 1.

282. "On with the Bill," 14 April 1986, *Daily Mail*.

283. "Lords' Day," 2 December 1985, *The Daily Telegraph*.

284. Patrick Wintour, "Pay Demands Threaten Shopping Bill," 10 December 1993, *The Guardian*; George Carey, speech to the House of Lords, 29 March 1994, in *Parliamentary Debates*, Lords, vol 553, cc. 988-990; for votes see Appendix 1.

285. Runcie, speech to General Synod, 3 July 1985, p. 555.

286. Carey, speech to Lords, 29 March 1994, c. 990.

287. Carey, *Know the Truth*, p. 193.

288. George Carey, speech to the House of Lords, 8 July 1997, in *Parliamentary Debates*, Lords, vol 581, c. 533.

289. Richard Brooks, "Churches Threaten New Year Boycott of Dome," 24 January 1999, *The Observer*.

290. "Archbishop of Canterbury Welcomes Research on Millennium Celebrations at the Dome," news release, 16 April 1999, http://web.archive.org/web/20021204030244/http://www.archbishopofcanterbury.org/releases/990416.htm.

291. National Secular Society, "Church and State," pp. 8-9.

292. Peter Brierley, ed., *UKCH: Religious Trends No. 7, 2007/2008: British Religion in the 21st Century* (London: Christian Research, 2008), pp. 4.2, 4.8.

293. Eric James, "York, the PM and the Church," 20 February 1983, *The Observer*; Stephen Bates, "How Williams Changed View on Splitting Church from State," 18 December 2008, *The Guardian*, http://www.guardian.co.uk/world/2008/dec/18/rowan-williams-disestablishment-new-statesman.

294. Runcie, speech at Kent University, 20 February 1981, p. 73.

295. Carey, speech at Lambeth Palace, 23 April 2002.

296. Williams, Q&A session at Westminster Abbey, 18 March 2008, "Holy Week: Faith & Politics Questions & Answers Session", http://www.archbishopofcanterbury.org/1715.

297. National Secular Society, "Church and State", pp. 42-44.

298. Davie, *Religion in Britain*, pp. 141-142.

299. "Runcie Would Retain the Law on Blasphemy," 11 January 1982, *The Guardian*.

300. Walter Schwarz, "Runcie Blasphemy Shift," 23 March 1990, *The Guardian*.

That recognised, it is also clear that this tended to be only a very minor motivation and that much archiepiscopal activity can be accounted for in other ways. Indeed, a very substantial amount – arguably most – of the Archbishop's political activity during this period cannot be explained by reference to institutional interests. The 1985 *Faith in the City* report, which was almost certainly the Archbishop's most high-profile entry into the political arena during this period, was sharply critical of both state and Church. Its recommendation that the Church Urban Fund be established was very expensive for the Church, and there is little evidence that it dramatically improved the Church's fortunes in urban areas. The Archbishop's outspoken defence of the rights of immigrants and criminals appears to have run counter to popular opinion and, in the case of the former, may have further eroded the Church's dominance of the religious 'sector' in England. Self-interest cannot explain why, at the precise moment when popular support for the government's handling of the Falklands crisis was highest, Runcie attracted the ire of the government and much of the media for the tone of his sermon at the thanksgiving service. Neither does self-interest appear to be a compelling explanation of the Archbishop's support for environmental concerns, despite the fact that he was broadly in line with popular opinion. Self-interest is particularly unconvincing in the case of Williams' lecture about sharia law, which attracted a firestorm of criticism from across the political spectrum and made for uncomfortable reading in the morning newspapers.

Thus, although institutional interests did influence the archiepiscopal contribution to politics during this period, they seem to have had a relatively minor and muted impact. Moreover, it is worth noting that almost every contributor to political debate has some institutional interests to protect. Even pressure and campaigning groups with generous and charitable goals need to maximise their own membership levels, resources, and social authority or capacity to influence. Accordingly, it is precisely *because* the Archbishop represents the institution of the Church that he has any influence in politics at all. It would be naïve to expect wholly disinterested political engagement from any actor. What is remarkable about the Archbishop's political activism is not that there is evidence of self-interest, but that there is so little of it, and that there are so many examples of political interventions that almost certainly cost the Archbishop goodwill and public sympathy.

> *Although institutional interests did influence the archiepiscopal contribution to politics during this period, they seem to have had a relatively minor impact.*

an outdated or unrepresentative voice?

The second objection is that the Archbishop's moral vision was outdated, or at least unrepresentative of the population at large. In chapter one, it was anticipated that this criticism would be particularly relevant to the cluster of issues often referred to as "traditional moral issues", namely those to do with sex and relationships and the sanctity of life. To an extent, the analysis in this report supports this anticipation. Williams' engagement with sanctity of life issues appears to have been particularly out of step with popular opinion, particularly on euthanasia and probably also on abortion and embryology. Some of Carey's comments on sex and sexuality are also vulnerable to this charge. Although probably not wildly unpopular at the time, his stances were nevertheless against the direction in which public opinion was travelling. That said, it is important to recognise that even in cases where the Archbishop was out of step with the population as a whole, he was nevertheless representative of a significant minority of public opinion.

Yet, even on the topic of traditional morality, there are also some surprising features of archiepiscopal political engagement. For a start, the Archbishop has not taken an unequivocally conservative stance on these issues, even when public opinion would have allowed him to. The best example is Runcie's decision to vote for a Lords amendment that would have weakened the impact of Section 28, which took place at a time when popular opposition to same-sex sexual relationships was very high. The same could be said of Carey's response to the Conservatives'"back to basics" campaign. Although Carey was the most vocal and conservative of the officeholders discussed on issues related to sex and relationships, he nevertheless drew a significant amount of criticism from some quarters of the press that felt he was not doing enough on these matters.

Moreover, the Archbishop was not especially active in these areas, as an analysis of his contribution to the Lords during this period shows. Excluding moments of mourning or celebration, internal Church operations, and the officeholders' introductions to the Lords, Runcie contributed to 15 Lords debates, Carey 10, and Williams 11. Of these, only Williams spoke in debates that were primarily about traditional moral issues (as defined in this report), once about euthanasia and once about human fertilisation and embryology legislation.

A slightly greater degree of activism is evident in their Lords votes. Once internal Church matters are excluded, Runcie cast 15 votes, Carey six and Williams three. Of these, three (20 percent) of Runcie's votes related to sanctity of life issues and one (7 percent) to Section 28. None of Carey's votes were about these traditional moral issues, and one (33 percent) of Williams' votes was about euthanasia. The picture of the Archbishop being obsessed by such issues, or throwing his weight around in the Lords to block every attempt at social liberalisation, is very far from the truth.

On other issues – including the response to urban poverty, climate change, British armed conflict, and Church schools – it appears that the Archbishop was in line with popular opinion. Moreover, when the Archbishop was out of line with public opinion, it was often about those issues that couldn't easily be considered as "outdated", such as when he defended the rights of asylum seekers and immigrants, or more restorative forms of justice.

Thus, while it is possible to argue that the Archbishop's political contribution was "outdated" this is not the criticism it might initially appear. Quite apart from anything else, "outdated" is often a matter of perspective. Runcie's appeal to statist remedies to urban deprivation was "outdated" to the architects of Thatcher's 'new right' economic policies, but not to the *Guardian* commentators who applauded *Faith in the City*. Conversely, Carey's interventions on marriage seemed "outdated" to social liberals but not to *Daily Mail* columnists. Moreover, not being in line with the majority view can hardly be said to constitute a reason to exclude someone from political debate, at least in a liberal, democratic society, a view voiced by even those who opposed (elements of) archiepiscopal politics. This was recognised by Lord Joffe, whose Assisted Dying for the Terminally Ill Bill was opposed by Williams:

> When the Church launched its campaign against my assisted dying Bill, my first instinct was to question its right to get involved but, when I thought of the many campaigns in which it has been involved – on urban deprivation, Make Poverty History, and numerous others in which it has done so much good – I saw that it was obviously right that it should be involved in campaigns on issues in which it believes.[1]

Overall, although the Archbishop's contribution can legitimately be called "unrepresentative" in a number of cases, this does little to undermine the value of his political comment.

Although the Archbishop's contribution can legitimately be called "unrepresentative" in a number of cases, this does little to undermine the value of his political comment.

an unnecessary or irrelevant voice?

The last of the three objections is that the Archbishop's stance was irrelevant or unnecessary. The evidence suggests that the Archbishop has very rarely been an entirely solitary moral voice in political debate, the only possible example to the contrary being the political earthquake following the publication of *Faith in the City*, and that being as much because the official opposition was in disarray as it was due to the content of the report itself. That said, there were a variety of other debates in which the Archbishop occupied an important position, such as with Runcie's activism in the Lords over the 1981 British Nationality Bill. In each of the policy topics considered in this report, the Archbishop's contributions have been considered significant enough to justify substantial coverage in the press.

Given the noisy and crowded debate that is modern politics, it would be naïve to expect the Archbishop to be a lone voice on any issue. However, while his actual stance was rarely distinctive, his reasons for adopting it often were. Critically, the fact that the

Archbishop based many of his political arguments explicitly on religious reasoning enabled him to rise above the political fray and draw attention to the wider moral dimensions of the issues. Such an approach allowed him to introduce Christian moral and theological perspectives into political debate, such as mankind's relationship with the earth and just war theory. In doing so, he also represented the perspective of an important and substantial constituency, practising and also, to an extent, nominal Christian believers and, to a lesser extent, those of other faiths.

In addition to this it appears likely that the institutional characteristics of the Church enhanced the value of the Archbishop's contribution to political debate by giving him access to particularly valuable information and perspectives. This is most clearly seen in the way that the first-hand experience of the clergy in urban areas, or in prisons, or in asylum centres helped shape the Archbishop's comments on urban deprivation, or criminal justice, or asylum and immigration policy. Likewise, the international connections of the Anglican Communion were drawn upon by Williams when approaching the topic of climate change.

The fact that the Archbishop is a religious leader also made him particularly sensitive to the religious dimensions to any political issue. This was particularly clear in Runcie's concern for the wellbeing of Britain's Muslim minority during the Gulf war, as well as the officeholders' comments on the implications of religious hatred legislation for minority religious groups. It was also evident in the cases of blasphemy legislation and the Christian character of religious education in schools – and, beneath the ensuing furore, in Williams' comments on sharia law. However much the Archbishop's position within political debate was replicated by other political actors (an inevitability in today's political culture), the reasons for his adoption of that position, both theological and empirical, were not so widely replicated, and as a result his contribution was far from being a mere duplication of other voices.

a moral voice for the common good?

It is arguable that these three objections do, to various extents and in different ways, diminish the value of the Archbishop's contribution to political debate in England over this period. Even so, the overwhelming conclusion has to be that the Archbishop did succeed in making a valuable contribution to political debate in support of the common good. This appears to be particularly clear for the first five topics considered. On urban poverty, the Archbishop was driven by a mixture of pastoral concern and theological conviction to promote the cause of the poorest in English society. The Archbishop's defence of the rights of immigrants and asylum seekers was at least partially motivated by what Carey described as "the moral responsibility, which is also a Christian duty, of welcoming the true asylum seeker who knocks on our door."[2] On criminal justice, the officeholders' support for better treatment of offenders – seemingly against the grain of public opinion – was motivated by a Christian understanding of the dignity of all human beings. When faced with the prospect of British armed conflict, the officeholders – particularly Runcie and Williams – turned to the moral criteria of just war theory. The Archbishop's concern for the environment and climate change was substantially motivated by two moral and theological values: right relationship with God's creation and right relationship with one another.

Even in the remaining three areas of policy, it seems likely that the Archbishop's stance was in large measure motivated by a moral concern for the common good. The case is probably strongest with respect to traditional moral values, on which topic the officeholders were motivated by their theological understandings of what it means to be authentically human, rather than by a desire to assert the authority of the Church, and still less to satisfy public opinion. Similarly, in the case of education policy, it is possible to understand the Archbishop's support of Church schools as subordinate to a wider vision for education policy that contests the all-too-widespread emphasis on developing the child's economic potential.

Perhaps not surprisingly, it is on religious policy that the Archbishop's political activism was most clearly motivated by the Church's institutional interests. Even here, however, institutional interests make weak explanations of some of the Archbishop's behaviour, most notably Williams' comments on sharia law. In many cases, it seems likely that the Archbishop's activity was heavily motivated by recognition of the spiritual dimensions of being human, as well as a sense of duty to represent the religious sector.

the future of archiepiscopal politics

Overall, the empirical evidence – of what the Archbishop said and the social and media context in which he said it – strongly suggests that over the last 30 years he has succeed in sounding a moral voice above the political fray that has at least been intended to draw attention to, and often succeeded in contributing to, the common good. This conclusion is important for at least two reasons. First, it supports the contention that arguments based on religious conviction can have value when

> *The empirical evidence strongly suggests that over the last 30 years he has succeed in sounding a moral voice above the political fray.*

deployed in the secular public square. In his Theos report, *Talking God,* Jonathan Chaplin argues that "religious public reasoning" is not only legitimate but in fact has the potential to enrich political debate.[3] The conclusion of this report supports his analysis. Second, given that some of the value of the Archbishop's moral contribution arose from the Church's established status, the report's findings have implications for the continued establishment of the Church of England.

The precise effect of establishment on the Archbishop's politics is debatable. It is argued by some that the positive effect of the Archbishop's political engagement is weakened by the Church's position as the state religion. Concluding their major study into the political involvement of the Church in the 1980s, Kenneth Medhurst and George Moyser suggest that "as long as the Church remains established, it will [...] be constrained to accept some pastoral responsibility for power holders. This, in turn, must set limits to its prophetic role." However, they indicate that the same would be true for any national church "whether legally established or not".[4] When asked about the capacity of an established Church to criticise the government, Carey responded, "there is a very real danger [...] that establishment can blunt the prophetic message because you have access, because you can talk it through in a civilised way."[5] Williams, by contrast, commented in an interview that "while there might be many reasons for watching what I say, being a nuisance to the people across the river [at the Houses of Parliament] is not a big consideration."[6] It seems likely that the Church's establishment does, to a small extent at least, limit the Church's capacity to criticise the government.

That said, disestablishment would surely weaken the Archbishop's political capacity in other respects. For a start, he would lose his automatic seat in the House of Lords. Although archiepiscopal voting in the Lords declined over this period, the Archbishop continues to use the Lords as a platform to make speeches about political matters, and as such the removal of his seat would almost certainly diminish his influence. Disestablishment would also deprive him of some of his access, although it is not likely that he would be left entirely out in the cold. It is possible that the Archbishop's sense of responsibility for the wellbeing of the nation would likewise be loosened, although again it seems highly unlikely that the Church would casually walk away from hundreds of years of commitment to the nation's wellbeing.

It is also probable that media attention to the Archbishop would diminish with disestablishment. Grace Davie points out that, prior to the publication of *Faith in the City* in 1985, other Christian denominations produced similar documents. They did not receive comparable media attention, and she takes this as evidence that "an established church can, it seems, still create an impact denied to other denominations".[7] More recently, Williams' speech about sharia law provoked substantial comment in the media. Stephen Monsma and Christopher Soper are almost certainly correct to conclude that "[t]he press coverage of Williams' proposal would simply not have been as extensive had he not been the most prominent spokesperson of the established Church of England."[8]

The appetite among the media for a respected moral spokesperson is considerable. Douglas Hurd, the former Home Secretary, only slightly exaggerated when he wrote that, "[i]f there were no Archbishop of Canterbury leading an established church, the media might well be pressing for us to create one".[9] On balance, it seems likely that the disestablishment of the Church would diminish the Archbishop's capacity to make a moral contribution to political debate.

None of this constitutes a clinching argument for establishment and the evidence discussed in this report is highly unlikely to persuade disestablishmentarians to change their mind. The nature of the archbishop's political interventions is only one factor among many – theological as well as political and sociological – that shape the debate about establishment. However, it is still a factor that demands careful attention. Ultimately, when considering the future establishment of the Church of England, the benefits brought by the Archbishop's participation in politics can only be a secondary concern. Moreover, if popular commitment to Christian belief in England continues to decline, the value of his contribution may likewise diminish. Yet the evidence analysed in this report suggests that, for now at least, the Archbishop retains an important capacity to enrich political debate. Were that capacity to be reduced, whether through disestablishment or any other means, national politics as a whole would be the poorer.

chapter 3 references

1. Lord Joffe, speech to the House of Lords, 19 May 2006, in *Parliamentary Debates,* Lords, vol 682, c. 553.

2. George Carey and Basil Hume, letter to editor, 13 November 1991.

3. Jonathan Chaplin, *Talking God: The Legitimacy of Religious Public Reasoning* (London: Theos, 2008).

4. Medhurst and Moyser, *Church and Politics,* p. 358.

5. Carey interview with author.

6. James Macintyre, "Interview," *New Statesman.*

7. Davie, *Religion in Britain,* p. 152.

8. Stephen V. Monsma and Christopher J. Soper *The Challenge of Pluralism: Church and State in Five Democracies,* Second edition (Lanham: Rowman & Littlefield, 2009), p. 144.

9. Douglas Hurd, "Reluctant Crusader: Runcie and the State," in *Runcie on Reflection: An Archbishop Remembered,* ed. Stephen Platten (Norwich: Canterbury Press, 2002), p. 28.

appendix 1: the archbishop's activity in the House of Lords

The research for this report has identified a total of 57 contributions in the House of Lords by the Archbishop during the period considered in this report. This figure comprises speeches in 54 debates (not counting multiple interventions on the same day about the same topic of debate), as well as the "introductions" of the three officeholders. For the purpose of this report, "debates" include all oral contributions to the Lords, including questions to government representatives. The list has been compiled by consulting the indexes for the final Hansard volume for each Lords session during this period. According to Andrew Partington's comprehensive study into the Lords Spiritual, during the Thatcher years (May 1979 – November 1990) Runcie made a total of 23 Lords contributions as Archbishop.[1] The research for this report has identified only 22. It is therefore possible that the list below is not exhaustive, although it almost certainly includes the vast majority of the Archbishop's Lords interventions during this period.

I: Introduction to the Lords E: Expressive of mourning or celebration
C: Internal Church of England matters
Source: Hansard

Date	Topic	Hansard reference	I	E	C
12/03/1980	Introduction	v. 406, c. 1069	X		
04/08/1980	Her Majesty The Queen Mother	v. 412, c. 1253-1254		X	
14/01/1981	The International Year of Disabled People	v. 416, cc. 65-69			
22/06/1981	British Nationality Bill	v. 421, cc. 875-878			
16/07/1981	Marriage of His Royal Highness The Prince of Wales to Lady Diana Spencer	v. 422, cc. 1370-1371		X	
20/10/1981	British Nationality Bill	v. 424, cc. 717-719			
04/02/1982	Brixton Disorders: The Scarman Report	v. 426, cc. 1412-1415			
14/04/1982	The Falkland Islands	v. 429, cc. 298-299			
20/05/1982	The Falkland Islands	v. 430, cc. 814-815			
22/06/1983	Address in Reply to Her Majesty's Most Gracious Speech	v. 443, c. 16			

Date	Topic	Hansard reference	I	E	C
15/11/1983	Crimes of Violence	v. 444, cc. 1154-1159, 1251			
11/04/1984	Prayer Book Protection Bill [H.L.]	v. 450, cc. 1214-1218			X
31/10/1984	Mrs. Ghandi: Assassination	v. 456, cc. 532-533		X	
29/10/1985	United Nations: 40th Anniversary	v. 467, cc. 1454-1459, 1525			
18/04/1986	Sunday Trading, Removal of Anomalies	v. 473, c. 877			
12/01/1987	Tributes to the late Lord Stockton	v. 483, cc. 359-361		X	
02/02/1987	Inner City Problems	v. 484, cc. 34-38			
03/05/1988	Education Reform Bill (Committee)	v. 496, cc. 510-512			
23/11/1988	Address in Reply to Her Majesty's Most Gracious Speech	v. 502, cc. 36-39			
03/07/1989	Clergy (Ordination) Measure	v. 509, cc. 1012-1016, c. 1037, cc. 1050-1053			X
17/07/1990	Her Majesty The Queen Mother: Humble Address	v. 521, c. 752		X	
06/09/1990	The Gulf	v. 521, cc. 1807-1810			
15/01/1991	The Gulf	v. 524, cc. 1097-1100			
24/04/1991	Introduction	v. 528, c. 261	X		
22/05/1991	Inner Cities: Neglect	v. 529, cc. 273-276			
10/06/1991	Care of Churches and Ecclesiastical Jurisdiction Measure	v. 529, c. 956			X
09/01/1992	Arab-Israeli Negotiations	v. 533, cc. 1651-1654			
03/02/1992	Further and Higher Education Bill [H.L.]	v. 535, c. 62			
12/05/1992	Address in Reply to Her Majesty's Most Gracious Speech	v. 537, cc. 259-262			
02/11/1993	Priests (Ordination of Women) Measure	v. 549, cc. 1001-1007			X
02/11/1993	Ordination of Women (Financial Provisions) Measure	v. 549, c. 1080			X
18/01/1994	Sudan	v. 551, cc. 576-579			
29/03/1994	Sunday Trading Bill (Committee)	v. 553, cc. 988-990			

Date	Topic	Hansard reference	I	E	C
12/05/1994	Tributes to the late Rt. Hon. John Smith MP	v. 554, c. 1650		X	
10/10/1994	Lord Shackleton: Tributes	v. 557, c. 703		X	
22/11/1994	Address in Reply to Her Majesty's Most Gracious Speech	v. 559, cc. 173-176			
06/11/1995	Tributes to the Late Yitzhak Rabin	v. 566, c. 1580		X	
05/07/1996	Society's Moral and Spiritual Well-being	v. 573, cc. 1691-1695, 1776-1778			
08/07/1997	Millennium Celebrations	v. 581, c. 533			
15/10/1999	Religions and International Order	v. 605, cc. 657-662, cc. 735-736			
13/07/2000	Her Majesty The Queen Mother	v. 615, cc. 378-379		X	
12/02/2002	Her Royal Highness The Princess Margaret	v. 631, cc. 993-994		X	
03/04/2002	Her Majesty Queen Elizabeth The Queen Mother	v. 633, cc. 392-393		X	
29/04/2002	The Queen's Golden Jubilee	v. 634, cc. 460-461		X	
12/03/2003	Introduction	v. 645, c. 1305	X		
26/03/2003	Children and Parents	v. 646, cc. 863-865			
06/10/2003	Tributes to the late Lord Williams of Mostyn	v. 653, cc. 7-8		X	
26/03/2004	Sentencing	v. 659, cc. 947-950, cc. 1002-1003			
02/02/2005	United Nations Reform, and Conflict in Africa	v. 669, cc. 256-259			
15/02/2006	Immigration Detention Centres	v. 678, c. 1151			
12/05/2006	Assisted Dying for the Terminally Ill Bill [H.L.]	v. 681, cc. 1196-1198			
19/05/2006	Churches and Cities	v. 682, cc. 501-506, cc. 567-570			
28/03/2007	Gambling (Geographical Distribution of Casino Premises Licences) Order 2007	v. 690, cc. 1677-1679			
15/01/2008	Human Fertilisation and Embryology Bill [H.L.]	v. 697, cc. 1185-1186			
06/02/2008	Young Offenders: Review of Restraint	v. 698, c. 1048			
25/04/2008	Families: Economic Inequality	v. 700, cc. 1768-1772, cc. 1827-1828			
12/02/2009	Children: Good Childhood Inquiry Report	v. 707, cc. 124/-1250			

The research for this report has identified a total of 25 votes by the Archbishop in the House of Lords during this period. They have been located by conducting an internet search (for "Canterbury, Abp.") for each of the relevant years of electronic Hansard records available at hansard.millbanksystems.com (1980-2005) and parliament.uk (1996-2010). These data have been cross-referenced against data that are available at publicwhip.org.uk (2001-2010). In common with Partington's research, 15 votes by Archbishop Runcie have been identified during the Thatcher years.[2]

Date	Legislation	Abp	Abp. vote	Lords vote
22/06/1981	British Nationality Bill	Runcie	Content	Not content
22/06/1981	British Nationality Bill	Runcie	Content	Not content
07/07/1981	British Nationality Bill	Runcie	Content	Not content
20/10/1981	British Nationality Bill	Runcie	Content	Not content
02/12/1985	Shops Bill	Runcie	Content	Not content
28/01/1987	Infant Life (Preservation) Bill	Runcie	Not content	Not content
01/02/1988	Local Government Bill	Runcie	Content	Not content
03/05/1988	Education Reform Bill	Runcie	Not content	Not content
05/05/1988	Education Reform Bill	Runcie	Content	Not content
05/05/1988	Education Reform Bill	Runcie	Not content	Not content
12/05/1988	Education Reform Bill	Runcie	Content	Content
17/05/1988	Education Reform Bill	Runcie	Content	Not Content
23/05/1988	Local Government Finance Bill	Runcie	Content	Not content
18/10/1990	Human Fertilisation and Embryology Bill	Runcie	Content	Not content
18/10/1990	Human Fertilisation and Embryology Bill	Runcie	Content	Not content
03/02/1992	Further and Higher Education Bill	Carey	Content	Not content
03/02/1992	Further and Higher Education Bill	Carey	Content	Content

Date	Legislation	Abp	Abp. vote	Lords vote
02/11/1993	Priests (Ordination of Women) Measure	Carey	Not content	Not content
29/03/1994	Sunday Trading Bill	Carey	Not content	Not content
29/03/1994	Sunday Trading Bill	Carey	Content	Not content
30/04/1996	Asylum and Immigration Bill	Carey	Content	Not content
13/04/1999	Sexual Offences (Amendment) Bill	Carey	Content	Content
25/01/2006	Terrorism Bill	Williams	Content	Not content
12/05/2006	Assisted Dying for the Terminally Ill Bill	Williams	Content	Content
28/03/2007	Gambling (Geographical Distribution of Casino Premises Licences) Order 2007	Williams	Content	Content

Source: Hansard

appendix 1 references

1. Partington, *Church and State,* p. 145.
2. Ibid., p. 97.

appendix 2: information about sources

Transcripts of some of Runcie's speeches are available in three published volumes, *Windows onto God*,[1] *One Light for One World*,[2] and *The Unity We Seek*.[3] Transcripts of some of Carey's early speeches are also available in a published volume, *Sharing a Vision*.[4] Many of Carey's later speech transcripts and press releases are available at an archive of his Archbishop of Canterbury website,[5] as well as at his current personal website (www.glcarey.co.uk). All press releases and speech transcripts relating to Williams are available through his website (www.archbishopofcanterbury.org). Newspaper content has been accessed through a variety of media, including the publications' websites, electronic databases such as NewsBank, and printed copies. Information can sometimes differ subtly (or, in some cases, substantially) between these media, and it is not always clear whether an article published online was also published in print.

appendix 2 references

1. London: SPCK, 1983.
2. London: SPCK, 1988.
3. London: Darton, Longman and Todd, 1989.
4. London: Darton, Longman & Todd, 1993.
5. Archive of www.archbishopofcanterbury.org, November 2002, at www.archive.org.